B*WITCHED

DESTINATION EVERYWHERE!
B*WITCHED ON THE ROAD

DESTINATION EVERYWHERE!
B*WITCHED ON THE ROAD

THE OFFICIAL TOUR BOOK

BILLBOARD BOOKS

First published in 1999 by Virgin Books
An imprint of Virgin Publishing Limited
Thames Wharf Studios
Rainville Road
London W6 9HT

First published in the United States in 1999 by Billboard Books,
an imprint of Watson-Guptill Publications, a division
of BPI Communications Inc., at 1515 Broadway, New York, NY 10036

Library of Congress Cataloging-in-Publication Data for this title
can be obtained from the Library of Congress.
Library of Congress Catalog Card Number: 99-65682
ISBN 0-8230-7855-8

Printed and bound by The Bath Press

Origination by Colourwise Ltd

Designed by Traffika Publishing Limited

Contents

Chapter 1
Flying High!

What a magical, memorable, mesmerizing year the four of us are enjoying...so much has happened that our feet have barely touched the ground!

Back in March we had our fourth British number one in a row with 'Blame It On The Weatherman.' We've spent our longest-ever period overseas touring in the USA. Recording is well under way for our second album and we are about to see a special dream come true – our very own B*Witched Tour.

*B*Witched – Destination Everywhere!* is our second official book. It gives us the chance to show you what life on the road is really like – from the sheer excitement of stepping out on stage before a live audience of thousands, to the times when all we wish for is our own bed and mam's home cooking!

It's been a tremendous experience and a great challenge putting this book together, especially as we seem to spend such little time in any one place. Our American schedule is often so hectic that we don't know which airport we're in, let alone which state or which time zone!

Our off-stage encounters with 'N Sync were few and far between

So, sit back, fasten your seatbelt, and prepare yourself for take-off into the topsy-turvy travel world of B*Witched!

B*Witched Review of '99

Our New Year began miles away from home on the west coast of the United States where we were booked for a string of performances supporting the American boy band 'N Sync. In fact, we had to cut short our Christmas holidays at home to be there, leaving on St. Stephen's Day for our first big American adventure.

We flew back to Britain in February to promote our fourth single 'Blame It On The Weatherman,' but were back in the States just before its official release date in March. We couldn't believe it when the song went straight to number one! Along with our three other number ones, 'C'est La Vie,' 'Rollercoaster' and 'To You I Belong,' it earned us a place in the *Guinness Book of Records* for the most successful debut by a girl band in the UK. We were over the moon!

It must have been about 7 a.m. in the States when our manager, Kim Glover, rang each of our hotel rooms to let us know that 'Weatherman' had topped the charts. We knocked on each other's doors, gave each other a hug and went back to bed as we were all so tired from the night before!

'...some of our most precious memories are of the different countries we have visited...'

As the year and century come to a close some of our most precious memories are of the different countries we have visited and of the wonderful new fans and friends we have made around the globe. Our music is there to make you happy and we hope we will continue to do so into the next millennium!

Blue-wigged babes at the BRIT Awards with fellow performers

We met the guys from 'N Sync for lunch that day and told them our fantastic news. When we went to our dressing room later on they'd done such a lovely thing, leaving chocolates and bunches of roses, and there was writing on a blackboard saying, 'Congratulations.' Thanks, guys, we really appreciated your gesture!

The whole situation was actually quite strange. There we were, just the four of us, far away from home, with another number one hit. We hadn't even seen any of our TV or promotions for 'Weatherman' with being away and our families weren't there to share our excitement. Actually, we've never properly celebrated our number ones and we must try and do it sometime!

During our 'Weatherman' promotion work we were invited to attend the BRIT Awards – a very important event in the music industry's calendar. Not only were we nominated in the Best International Newcomer category, but we also got to perform in the now famous Abba medley along with Billie, Cleopatra, Steps and Tina Cousins.

Our outfits were fabulous – very 'Abbaesque' – and had been created especially for the event by our own stylists. We all had a colour theme – ours was blue, based on Abba's 'Waterloo' costumes. We wore big platform shoes and bright blue wigs and only had about three hours to rehearse the routine. Fortunately we knew a lot of the lyrics from singing Abba songs years ago at karaoke! Before we went on stage we all said a big group prayer, then it was showtime!

The medley tied in with the opening of a new West End musical, *Mamma Mia!*, which features many of Abba's songs. Bjorn Ulvaeus from Abba was in the audience and said he was delighted with the job we did when we met him after the performance. There were loads of press people there and we did lots of interviews afterwards. We'll never forget that night!

After returning to the States early in March it was almost two and a half months before we hit home territory again. We managed to get a few days off in the middle of May to see our families and friends back in Ireland. In England we did a book signing for our first official book, then we were US-bound once again.

As our second album is due to be released in the UK, Europe and the States at the end of October, we've been recording whenever we can, wherever we can. Some tracks have been recorded in the UK, others in the US. We also used Bryan Adams' studio in Vancouver, Canada, while we were in the city to attend the Youth Awareness Awards.

Video footage for the first single off the album, 'Jessie Hold On,' was shot on location near San Diego. It has a country feel — very up-tempo, with some banjo — which makes everyone want to get up and dance. Our video director wanted to film at an authentic Western railway station, with a real steam train, but it was impossible to find the right location in Britain. That's why we headed for America's deep West and what an incredible experience it was!

We dressed up as engine boys in the video. We usually put glitter on people's faces, but for this one Lindsay went around putting muck on everyone's faces — it was really funny!

From the beginning of the year we've had one very special project bubbling away at the back of our minds — our very own tour. It's a dream come true and we intend to give it our heart and soul! Shanie, our choreographer, remained with us in the States from the end of July to start rehearsals for the

The day we were leaving England we were booked to attend the Ivor Novello Awards, for which 'C'est La Vie' had been nominated in two categories — Best Song Musically and Lyrically and Best-Selling UK Single. It was all a bit embarrassing because we had to leave to catch our flight about five minutes after the second nomination was announced. It probably looked as if we'd walked out because we hadn't won an award, but we genuinely had a plane to catch!

Our time in America has been spent performing in a vast array of venues from shopping malls to indoor theatres and huge arenas. We've taken part in radio road shows, have appeared on national TV networks and have slotted in countless press interviews.

November dates. We want ours to be different from any other tour and so have lots of surprises in store. We don't want to give too much away, but let's just say our fans will definitely know they've been to a B*Witched concert!

Secrets of Success

LINDSAY

To look at our schedule and to have the will to go through with it, you have to love and want the job very much! We are all naturally determined and have never been scared of hard work.

We look after ourselves, take our vitamins, go to bed early and stay focused. It's too easy to get side-tracked in this business! Thanks to our efforts our dreams are being fulfilled day by day.

SINÉAD

This year has been a complete whirlwind! The expectations of going to America were all in the distance and then suddenly we were there. Sometimes I find it difficult to put into words just how excited I feel.

I think the secret of our success has been a mixture of our recording company, Sony, believing in us and of us working hard, believing in our dreams and never giving up on them.

KEAVY

Our success has a lot to do with our drive, determination and teamwork right from the beginning. We met three years ago in Dublin and danced our hearts out at the Digges Lane dance centre. We wrote our own songs and put all our savings towards helping make our dreams of performing come true. We would work through the day and rehearse at night – there was never any argument about it.

EDELE

I don't think that all that's happened to us recently has changed me as a person, but certainly I've grown up. In the past year we've travelled the world and met so many people. I never imagined we would go so far, so quickly! If you read our schedule on paper it looks a lot more hectic than it feels during the day. Sometimes we don't even get time to read it!

B*WITCHED – THE CHART TOPPERS
UNITED KINGDOM

SINGLES

Song title	Release date	Best chart position
C'est La Vie	May 1998	1
Rollercoaster	September 1998	1
To You I Belong	December 1998	1
Blame It On The Weatherman	March 1999	1
Jessie Hold On	October 1999	?

ALBUMS

Song title	Release date	Best chart position
B*Witched	October 1998	3
Awake and Breathe	October 1999	?

UNITED STATES

SINGLES

Song title	Release date	Best chart position
C'est La Vie	December 1998	9
Rollercoaster	May 1999	69
Blame It On The Weatherman	August 1999	?

ALBUMS

Song title	Release date	Best chart position
B*Witched	March 1999	12
Awake and Breathe	October 1999	?

Chapter 2
Globe-Trotters

USA — Here We Come!

Among the many exciting places we've been to, we've spent a lot of time in America. The door opened for us at the end of '98 when we did a showcase for Sony, our record company, in New York. 'N Sync's promoter was at the showcase and it all started from there. So we were soon in the US promoting ourselves and working hard.

Before our first live performance of the tour, we were warned not to expect too big a reception because the audience was there to see a boy band. But we got a great reaction and were delighted. Our album *B*Witched* (Epic label) had not yet been released in the States, but 'C'est La Vie' was starting to get played on the radio and some of the kids were singing along.

The chart system in the US is different from the UK in that eighty per cent of the figures are based on radio play and it's obviously very difficult to get on to every single radio station in America. So we were pleasantly surprised when American

audiences really liked us! Meanwhile, 'C'est La Vie' reached the Top Ten of the Billboard Top 100 Chart and was certified Gold.

Our album, which was released in March, went Platinum (that's one million copies sold) and peaked at number 12 in the Billboard Top 200 Album Chart. Sales were boosted by a Disney In-Concert Special we filmed at Disneyland, California. It was aired at least ten times, sometimes twice a day. Over 742,000 households tuned in!

SINÉAD

I think people take to us very easily, not just because of our image, but because our music is so uplifting and happy. And the Irish theme in our songs has been a big favourite in the States – definitely an extra bonus for the Americans. There isn't much pop music in America at the moment, so we came in at a really good time. We have something just a bit different to offer: our Irish music in pop! And people also like the way our music is positive and very happy.

KEAVY

Most of our performances in the States have been live, which is so exciting – there's always a new audience and someone seeing you for the first time. I'm always a bit nervous before going on stage, but I have such a good time when I'm out there that I soon forget any nerves.

What I feel most is sheer excitement. Just looking at all those smiling faces looking at you makes the job so worthwhile.

B EDELE

We've performed before audiences from 4,000 to 18,000 across the USA and had such a warm reception wherever we've been. It's so rewarding when parents come up to us and say what great role models we are for their kids. We never feel any pressure about being role models, which is great. They love the fact that we wear denim, which is easy to wear and affordable to copy. Most kids have a pair of denims at home for a start. The parents say they listen to our music too – what a wonderful seal of approval!

LINDSAY

We know how difficult it is to break into the American market, so it's been an added bonus to do so well there. As well as performing in theatres and arenas from coast to coast, we have made several shopping mall appearances. One that we did, in Long Island, really sticks in my mind. I don't think we were prepared for how many people were going to be there. We came out on the top floor of this mall and had to get down to a lower level by escalator. As we descended we could see that the whole mall was jammed with people. It was such a nice feeling – people were there just to see us. That's when I finally felt that we'd been recognized in the US!

First Impressions

What can we say? Everything about America is BIG! You ask for a coffee and get a huge cup. You ask for a drink and get a HUGE glass. It can be annoying, because sometimes all you want is a small drink, in a small glass! Even the portions of food are enormous.

American people are extremely outgoing. You always get a chatty waiter in a restaurant to make you feel really comfortable. Wherever we go, we get good service with a smile!

We'd had visions of New York and Los Angeles being very glamorous cities. In fact, they were not as big as we thought and, like most cities, were very noisy. When we arrived in New York for the first time we were quite jet-lagged. Unfortunately, Lindsay and Keavy were woken by New York city noises around 5 a.m. and ended up going round the shops before anyone else had surfaced!

The more we travel across America, the more we can see just how different each state is from the next. They are like completely different countries! As much as we enjoy visiting all these new places, none of us would really like to live in the States permanently, although it might be different if our families lived there. At the end of the day there's no place like home!

It didn't take us long to pick up a few American expressions and some new words. We probably all say '*mawl*' now for mall. Chips are what we'd call crisps back home. Instead of saying, 'Let's go to the cinema or the pictures,' we now say 'movies'. We ask for tomato sauce whereas the Americans say ketchup and if you want *still* water, we've learned to ask for spring water or water without bubbles or no air.

And of course in some states, they might have different words for things from the state you've just been in. You just think you've cracked it and then in the next state, you find yourself not being understood all over again! If only we could cast a B*Witched spell on the American language, then we'd have no problems!

All Aboard the Magic Bus!

It's a mad, mad, world on the road with B*Witched! Our fast-moving daily schedule is definitely not for anyone lazy.

The B*Witched tour bus – our second home!

In the many weeks we've spent in America already this year, we've visited almost every state and travelled thousands of miles.

Some days we have to take up to four flights a day to meet our commitments. We totally lose track of what time or what day it is!

But when we're not jetting here, there and everywhere, our main means of getting around is our truly amazing tour bus – a huge 40ft silver Prevost. This cuts out the need for cars and taxis, allows us to sleep between venues, has cooking facilities and a lounge area where we can all chill out, chat or watch TV.

Step on board and you're in the dining area, which has a fridge, freezer and microwave. There's a toilet on the left, then you walk on down through a door where we've twelve bunk beds. Some of this area is used for hanging our clothes. At the far end of the bus is our sitting room, equipped with satellite TV, video and stereo. The only thing the bus doesn't have is a shower, but that's never really a problem as most nights we stay in a hotel anyway.

We always make sure we bring along some good old Irish cheese and onion crisps, which are the best in the world!

C'est la Vie on board the tour bus!

Sinéad relaxes with the tour bus teds!

One special furry friend is our Tour Teddy, Miller. He was named after an old man we met when we stopped for petrol once. When our soundmen told him that we were singers, he said he'd written some songs for Roger Miller back in the 80s. After meeting him we named a dark brown teddy Miller and a furry rabbit, Roger.

Our tour crew includes Jeff, the bus driver, who has Hungarian roots, but has lived in America all his life. He has long blond hair and always wears a cap and he's always got a story to tell. Jeff used to drive for big male rock bands like Guns'N'Roses and Black Sabbath, so when he heard he was to be driving a young girl band like B*Witched, you can imagine his reaction!

Miller, the official tour teddy bear

Manhattan popcorn is wonderful too and we all love microwave popcorn.

The bus is crammed with teddy bears, which have been given to us by fans. After we've finished a tour, we like to pass on all of the teddy bears to a children's hospital or charity of some sort.

Marian Neill is our Scottish wardrobe lady and she always has a lot of work to do. What would we do without her? She looks after our clothes, washes and irons, gets food out of the canteen to have on the bus and goes shopping. Marian has a lovely personality and is always giggling. She's worked with a lot of bands and is well used to Irish people and our sense of humour — especially when we are slagging her Scottish accent!

Our Tour Manager, Wilf Wright, is English, but has lived in America for many years and has loads of experience in the music business. His job is basically to look after us and make sure everything is running smoothly. He knows how to draw the line between having a good laugh and being serious. When we cover the soundmen in glitter before a gig (one of our pre-performance rituals), Wilf would never go so far as to wear it too. He's usually got lots of important people to deal with so he can't afford to look ridiculous!

Last, but not least, there are the sound guys, Steve Luttley and Jim Ebdon, who are both English and have worked together for the past two years. Other artists they've worked with include Gary Barlow, Natalie Imbruglia and Conner Reeves.

They're always a great laugh and good fun to have around, but at the end of the day they take their work very seriously and are perfectionists in everything they do. Steve mixes the sound for our in-ear monitors which enable us to control the level of the music while we're performing, whereas Jim mixes the sound for the audience.

They bring all the sound gear along in two big road cases. They're virtually self-contained and all they need at the other end is a good PA system.

Show Time!

We get used to being thrown in at the deep end and that's exactly what happened when we joined the 'N Sync tour! People often ask us how we manage to sing and dance so energetically at the same time. Well, we've just had to get used to it and learn how to control our breathing as we go along.

During one trip back to Britain we were given some breathing exercises by a lady called Mary Hammond and we'll be working with her more before our own tour. Most of our live performances in the States lasted twenty minutes. Our own concerts will be nearer an hour and a quarter long, which is a big difference. We are always open to suggestions and are grateful for any tips we are given on breathing. We are already benefiting from having been told to stress the end of certain words to help us get our breath more easily for the next line.

Edele wonders who has taken mike Number Three

As for our dancing, we don't get much chance to rehearse between gigs and would probably only do so if we were going to introduce a new routine. Once in a blue moon our choreographer, Shanie, will fly out to see how we're doing. If we look at all sloppy, then he'll say, 'Right, in the studio tomorrow,' and we'll spend a couple of hours tidying everything up!

SINÉAD

Every venue is different and so are our dressing rooms. Some might be quite big, with a leather couch, others might consist of a tiny room with no hot water! But if we're really in a rush then we get changed on the tour bus. Our denim stage clothes will have been washed and ironed beforehand by Marian, then it's just a question of finishing make-up and hair. Finally we do a physical and vocal warm-up.

We usually do our own make-up as we like to keep it fairly natural and we don't really do anything special because we're going to be under stage lights. For some TV specials or video shoots, our make-up artist, Lee Pearson, will fly out to join us.

I don't really have any major preferences as regards the type of clothes I wear, but I kind of like three-quarter length trousers and slash-neck tops for performing in the States as it gets so warm and that way I feel I'm getting a bit of air.

I simply don't have time to get nervous before we go on, but I do hate it if we have to stand about in the wings. Excitement is the main emotion you feel. We know our routine so well now that we're on automatic pilot and might only get nervous if we'd changed it in some way.

I'd worked in the theatre before I was with B*Witched and thought that theatre audiences were big, but it was nothing compared to the atmosphere you get when you step out on stage in a large arena. It's just mindblowing – you get such an adrenalin rush!

KEAVY

We basically have three or four different outfits on tour, which have been created by our stylist, Faye Sawyer, who knows exactly what we want. For example, Edele always has to have a pair of flares and Lindsay usually likes baggy trousers. Sinéad and I are not too bothered and will wear whatever. One set of costumes we refer to as *'Rosie O'Donnell'* as this is what we wore when we appeared on her TV show.

Sound man Jim Ebdon tries to give Edele some computer lessons!

We try to arrive at a venue about an hour before we go on, which gives us time for our physical and vocal warm-up. I like to touch up my make-up then chill out for a few minutes. I get panicky if there are a lot of people around making a fuss!

If a venue doesn't have any dressing rooms then we might end up getting changed in someone's office! In our dressing room we normally like to have lots of water, raw vegetables, fruit, soft drinks, our vitamin tablets and, very important, pretzels!

It's also essential to have lots of water when we're on stage. The climate in the States is generally much warmer than we are used to and we really notice the difference with our breathing. We always try to get a quick drink of water between songs, although Sinéad somehow always manages to get at least ten gulps!

After a performance the first thing I have to do is wash my feet! If I can take a shower, great, otherwise I just must wash my feet. I love getting into clean clothes, getting back on to the tour bus and just relaxing. We never get much time to spend with the bands we perform with as we're usually coming off stage when they're about to go on and then we're heading straight off to the next destination.

Sometimes we go out for something to eat, but whatever we do, we like to have a chat about the show we've just done and whether anything went wrong. We always wait for Jim and Steve to let us know how it went from a sound point of view. Usually, after a gig, we're all still so excited we just want to talk about everything.

Two young girls ended up in our US 'Rollercoaster' video and when we saw the outside of their house, we couldn't resist a photo

EDELE

We always try and eat no later than two and a half hours before a performance. If we haven't got that much time to spare then we'll eat afterwards. It's so important to eat properly, but it's not always possible. I remember when we were in Australia, we'd just performed at the Sydney Opera House and were rushing to get to a radio interview. We managed to grab a sandwich to eat in the car on the way, but it was horrible, so we ended up having a bowl of soup while we were doing the interview! It's definitely not good for you to eat lunch while you're running around.

Are we superstitious? Well, I'm very superstitious. We have a number of rituals we have to go through before a performance, which includes putting glitter on the soundmen. Twice we didn't and each time something went wrong!

Also, if someone gives us ankle bracelets, then we can't take them off until they break off – they're kind of good luck charms. I remember one bracelet kept digging into my leg while I was dancing. It was killing me, but I wouldn't take it off!

In the same way as Keavy likes to wash her feet straight after a show, I have to clean my teeth just before we go on! Another thing is that I always have to have microphone no. 3. If for some reason that's not possible then I have to get a sticker with the number three to put on the mike.

Before we go on stage all four of us wish each other good luck, give each other a hug and say a prayer. But our hugs have to be in order! I will hug Lindsay, Sinéad and then Keavy; Lindsay hugs Edele, then Keavy, then Sinéad; Keavy hugs Sinéad, then Lindsay, then Edele and Sinéad hugs Keavy, then Edele, then Lindsay. Got that? Maybe it's the twin sister thing, but Keavy and I have to have the last hug – if anyone else tries to give us a hug at the last minute, we have to find each other and hug again! Also, when we are having a drink and say, Cheers!, Keavy and I always have to say it to each other last and we must take a drink from the glass.

LINDSAY

I always have to jump up and down before I get in gear to go on stage. I always check my shoelaces and tie a double bow so I don't trip up on them, which has happened before.

I do my hair as soon as I get out of the shower, put in some mousse and scrunch it dry, which is easy for me because my hair's naturally curly. My make-up then only takes about fifteen minutes. I prefer to wear baggy clothes – I sometimes feel restricted in a tight pair of jeans and baggy clothes are much easier for bending down and sitting on the floor. As our routines are so energetic, I prefer to wear a nice little top to keep cool.

Backstage I get a real adrenalin rush – I'm always just so anxious to get out there. All this touring has definitely been good preparation for our own tour – we've really got a taste of what it's like to be on the road.

Koala cuddles Down Under

We've only been doing about a twenty-minute set. Our concerts on our own will be well over an hour long and will test our stamina more, so that means we'll be spending a lot of time in the gym before November!

On the Move

Touring has taken up the majority of our time during recent visits to the States, including playing the opening of the Women's World Cup Soccer Tournament, performing at the new *Cosmopolitan* magazine, *Cosmo Teen*, launch party and taking part in the mid-summer *Nickelodeon 'All That Tour'*.

We managed to enjoy some beautiful weather while performing outdoors at several radio road shows and we appeared live on KTLA Morning TV News as well as being guests on *The Tonight Show with Jay Leno*, *The View*, the *Rikki Lake Show*, *Rosie O'Donnell*, *Fox Kids Network*, *Regis & Kathy Lee* and the *Donny & Marie Show*.

We wrote and recorded a theme song for an upcoming Disney animated series, *Sabrina the Teenage Witch*, and were expected to guest-star on the show this summer. With video director Paul Andresen, we shot a new version of our 'Rollercoaster' video for the US market and had these gorgeous denim and suede outfits designed for us by our stylist, Faye. She's the best!

We got to hold a possum in Australia

Our third US single, 'Blame It On the Weatherman,' was released in August and there is a B*Witched home video available out there. It's called *We Four Girls Are Here To Stay* and includes a collection of our hit videos, some live performances and interviews.

We've been featured in pop and teen magazines across the nation and have been delighted with all the reviews. Some days we can have up to ten press interviews. Not many journalists get the chance to interview us all at once — it's a question of grabbing us when they can on a mobile phone while we are travelling from A to B.

Audiences have ranged from two years old to fifty-two and we've received a fantastic reception wherever we've been. And even grandmothers have come up to us and said what great role models we are for their grandchildren!

Down Under and All That

We're all agreed that one of the nicest places we've visited is Australia and we can't wait to take our own tour there in the New Year!

The people were very friendly. Australians have a similar sense of humour to the Irish and they are very laid back! You could call it Ireland in the sunshine!

'C'est La Vie' had done really well already and getting to perform in the Sydney Opera House was just unbelievable! We've always wanted to hold a Koala and we had our photo taken with one while we were there, as well as with a possum and a kangaroo – they were so cute!

We only spent three days in New Zealand and that's a fabulous place too. We really didn't want to leave. It was strange that we were so far away from home and that people knew us. Thousands of people were at some of the 'in-store' signings. We had to cancel one because so many people turned up and we didn't want anyone to get hurt. Even the fire department felt it would be hazardous to go ahead!

Having a ball Down Under!

Japan was another fascinating country to visit. Again, we didn't spend more than a few days there, but we received a very warm welcome. Our most vivid memory is of the grasshopper we ate. Keavy felt sick for days afterwards, just thinking about it!

We had to dress up in authentic Japanese kimonos for a TV crew to shoot us shopping in Tokyo. They gave us socks, which are stitched so that your big toe is separated from the others, to wear with the traditional wooden sandals. Boy, were they uncomfortable!

One of the TV crew filming us decided we should hang on to this wonderful Japanese lantern we'd found in one of the shops. The police followed us back to our hotel thinking we had stolen it. It was hilarious and luckily we had left it with the guy from the TV station. You can imagine the look on our manager's face when the police turned up!

We had a stop-over in Bangkok en route to Australia and that's definitely a place we'd all like to return to. Just the shops in the airport made us want to go back — they were really interesting and very original.

We've had a great time in Europe too and look forward to going back soon. We've got a great following there. Cultures may be very different around the world but, at the end of the day, our fans all have one thing in common — they support us with equal enthusiasm and give us a warm welcome wherever we go.

TRAVEL FACT FILE
EDELE CLAIRE
CHRISTINA EDWINA LYNCH

Nationality: Irish.

Star sign: Sagittarius.

Distinguishing marks: The scar between my eyebrows.

Hair colour: Black now, but naturally it's brown.

Eyes: Blue/green.

Height: 5ft 6in.

Shoe size: 5½.

Countries visited: America, all of Europe, Australia, New Zealand, Japan and Singapore.

Favourite foreign expression: 'How you going!' It's Australian and sounds cool when they say it in their accent!

First trip overseas: I went on a family trip to Portugal by plane.

Most interesting country visited: Japan, it's so different to the way we live.

Favourite means of transport: If it's a long journey, then our tour bus because you can sleep in a bed as you travel.

Worst ever travel experience: My bag fell off the baggage train and I ruined all my clothes.

Funniest travel story: We arrived at one of our first gigs on the local bus.

Best foreign food: I love Chinese.

Worst foreign food: They don't have great food in Germany.

Favourite city: Dublin – there's no place like home!

Ideal holiday location: I'd love to visit Africa or spend time on a tropical island.

Have you ever been badly sunburned, or bitten by anything while on holiday? I was bitten by a spider fish in the sea and the lifeguards used some special spray as my leg was really swollen.

Do you approve of topless bathing? Everyone to their own.

Do you wear a bikini or a one-piece? A bikini is nice for sunbathing but a one-piece is better if you're swimming.

What kind of suitcase do you use? A hard Carlton suitcase – they're really handy.

What's the secret to 'travelling light'? I wish I knew!

Flight bag essentials: Hand cream and moisturizer.

What would you be most embarrassed for a custom's officer to see in your suitcase if there was a baggage check? Perhaps my 'smalls,' although I'm sure they've seen it all before!

Do you collect travel souvenirs? I usually collect the laminates from shows.

Do you have a driver's licence? Only a provisional.

Who are better drivers, men or women? I think women have more patience!

Most unusual form of transport taken: Being pulled along on ice by a rope attached to the back of a van!

Any means of transport which you'd like to use? Concorde – it would get me to my destination much quicker.

If you were shipwrecked and washed-up on a desert island, who would you want as your companion and which three possessions would you like to have: I couldn't pick just one person. I think I could survive with my Discman, an umbrella and lots of drinking water!

Chapter 3

Wish You Were Here...

Being a pop star sounds very glamorous to many people, but coping with a gruelling schedule of tour dates, flights and bus journeys is very hard work. It's both physically and mentally demanding.

One glance at our diary dates and you'll see that days off are few and far between, although we did all enjoy a two-week summer holiday this year – our first proper break since B*Witched hit the music scene! Our schedule might say we have so many days off ahead of us, but this can change at the last minute. This makes it difficult to plan our free time in advance, so all we can do is take every day as it comes.

Whether it's a few hours, a day or a long weekend, our time off is therefore extremely precious. When we are far away from home, we like to spend our days together – mainly because we are such close friends and have so much in common. Read on and you'll discover how we try to unwind and relax...

KEAVY

How do I relax? Well, I like to sleep a lot and not wake up! Straight after an evening gig we'd probably get something to eat in catering or go to a restaurant or back to the tour bus to watch a film, or just chill out in the hotel we're booked into. My favourite actors are Mel Gibson and Meg Ryan and my favourite TV programme just has to be *Friends*.

If we have a free day in New York or LA then we'll probably go shopping together. I always head straight to the Tommy Hilfiger section or the Diesel shop in New York. If I see something I like, then I've got to have it! It's nice to have casual clothes and to dress up, so I do buy both. The thing about being in our business is that people expect us to look good all the time. You never know who's going to be taking a photograph or when, so I suppose we all try to look our best, at all times.

And, of course, compared to our pre-B*Witched days, it's nice to be able to shop without worrying too much about the cost. Also, due to the exchange rates, clothes shopping has been much cheaper for us in the States.

I don't enjoy shopping in New York as much as I do in LA because it's so noisy and busy. Sinéad is definitely the shopaholic out of all of us – she could spend a whole day in a shoe shop! As for me, I have a thing about chemists. I just love going into chemists and looking around. I'll buy anything from scissors and shampoo to hair bobbins! My favourite scent is *Jean Paul Gaultier for Men* and my favourite beauty product is *Aveda* foundation.

I should really buy souvenirs of all the places we've visited. I've always meant to, but never do. I did start to buy badges as a memento, but it became too much hassle. In Japan I bought kimonos, some dolls, coasters and a scroll.

If we're not shopping, then we might take the opportunity to lounge around the hotel pool, usually listening to music. My favourite CD of the moment is by my favourite male solo artist Conner Reeves. I also like Whitney Houston.

If the weather is warm and we get the chance to sunbathe, then I always wear some kind of sun protection cream and it's always a good idea to put extra conditioner in your hair. It's so important to look after your skin, but I'd never go so far as to have cosmetic surgery. You are what you are and I'm happy with the way I am!

We always have separate hotel rooms, which means we all have our own 'space.' Even though we get along so well, it's nice to have your own room to go back to.

If we decide to eat out, then my first choice is seafood. I adore lobster, but I don't get to eat it too often. I don't eat red meat, but love chicken. My favourite drink is water — I know it's boring, but that's the truth! *Benihana's* is one of the best restaurants I've been to. They have them in the US and England. The table you dine at is around a cooker where you watch them create this amazing food. We try not to eat fast food, although I'd recommend the *Boston Market* in the States, which serves fast, but 'proper' food.

I never think about putting on weight when I'm eating out. You should never compare yourself to anyone else. Everyone is built differently. The way you are is the way you are meant to be. If you eat properly all the time then you shouldn't have a problem.

EDELE

One of the nicest and most memorable days we had off while on tour in the States was in Atlanta. Our bus driver knew an idyllic lakeside location. The four of us and the crew rented a jet-ski for the day, went out to one of the little islands and made a BBQ. It was heaven!

My first choice for relaxing would be to sit by the hotel pool.

I prefer shopping in a street to a mall – they're far too big. There's never enough time to see everything and you're rushing around so much, you actually miss what you want. I picked up a couple of nice things for my summer holiday in Vancouver, which is a beautiful city. When you're not spending Irish money or sterling, it's far easier for you to spend – foreign currency is almost like toy money. And a credit card is very dangerous – I prefer using cash!

I don't buy souvenirs but do like to keep laminates or flyers from the shows we've done. Collecting too many souvenirs might cause a real problem with packaging. During my summer holiday this year I bought a really unusual mirror with horses in a kind of relief in the centre. It's very heavy and very breakable and I had no idea how I was going to get it back home, but I couldn't resist it!

We don't have restrictions as such placed on us by our record company with regard to taking part in dangerous activities and I'm a bit of a scaredy-cat anyway. But Keavy and Sinéad once heard about a parachute jump going on round the corner from our hotel and were dying to have a go. At the last minute they thought they'd better check with our record company. The answer was no!

I like to listen to all kinds of music – it's very influential – although I especially like The Corrs, TLC and Shania Twain. My favourite song of all time has to be *Eternal Flame* by the Bangles.

If I'm sunbathing I always make sure I have cream on from head to toe and always put a higher factor on my face and shoulders. I like to avoid strap marks because they look awful if you're wearing a nice top. Oh, and I drink plenty of water when I'm in the sun.

Like my sister, I love seafood, especially shellfish and especially lobster! I love the taste and I love spending time getting it out of the shell - mmmm! I tried an oyster once, but never again!

That B*Witched cat gets everywhere!

LINDSAY

At the end of a really hectic day I like to unwind by looking around where we are staying or listening to music or just being by myself. Mariah Carey, Bon Jovi, TLC, Bryan Adams, George Michael are all favourites. I've got a Discman and loads of CDs. I also love going bowling or to the cinema. I adored *Titanic* because it was so romantic. Brad Pitt and Meg Ryan are my favourite actors.

If I get a whole day off I prefer to go out walking or looking round the shops and have lunch out. If the sightseeing is interesting then I'd do that.

Trousers are my weakness when it comes to clothes shopping – I must have at least fifty pairs! Some of the big American stores like Bloomingdales are not that much different from the stores back home. We never get much hassle with people recognizing us – not even back home. The odd person will come up and say something or maybe ask for an autograph, but as a rule they leave us alone.

If we're dining out, I like seafood, Italian, Chinese, whatever. I'm not very fussy about food. I'm quite adventurous really, although I hate really hot food like chilli. I want to enjoy my food without turning red! Something I really enjoy, which we cook at the apartment, is chicken ragout and spaghetti.

Being half Greek (my dad's Greek and my mum's Irish) I love many Greek dishes. I lived in Greece until I was thirteen, so it's hardly surprising! My favourite dish would be pastichio, a pasta dish a bit like lasagne, with meat and bechamel sauce. And I love moussaka – a meat dish with aubergines and tomatoes, topped with cheese sauce. I prefer to drink fresh juices but do have an occasional fizzy drink. I don't have any sporting hobbies. I was much more into sport when I was at school and liked games like volleyball, netball and rackets, although we have started to go to the gym regularly to prepare for our tour.

SINÉAD

I think that in general we have had more time off than ever this year. Each time we come back from the States it's not for a holiday, but to recuperate! America overall has been like a holiday for us because we enjoy performing live so much, although the pace can be quite stressful.

We never really plan what we are going to do after a gig. We might go and have dinner or go for a drink or a walk around. I quite like going to the gym or having a massage to unwind. I'm into homeopathic treatments and collect aromatherapy oils. You can't beat a relaxing bath with lavender oil.

Given half the chance, I'd probably go shopping on a day off. Because we don't sometimes shop for months on end we have to make up for it! Vancouver is my favourite city for shopping – they have such lovely things there. It's very like London or Dublin, with lots of good restaurants, bars and cafés. Shop assistants in the States are generally very polite. They all say, 'Hello, can I help you?' and usually introduce themselves by their first name as well.

I love buying black and baby blue clothes. Black because it's so classy and sophisticated, baby blue because it's subtle. I tend to buy more dressy things and I love high heels and sandals. Before B*Witched I used to be much more careful when shopping. I can afford to buy certain things now, although I do feel guilty sometimes. Our tour manager put me at ease once and said because we all work so hard, we can do this, and not to feel bad about it.

It still feels good to get a bargain and I'm very proud of a Prada belt I bought for half-price back home. I bought loads of souvenirs in Japan, LA and Australia – nothing major, just lots of little bits.

Keavy, Edele and Lindsay get recognized far more easily than I do – I never get hassled. I flew Aer Lingus a while back and didn't have my Gold Circle Card with me to get into the business class lounge. The girl on the door asked me for my card and I didn't like to say who I was so that she'd let me in! She certainly didn't recognize me and I would never take advantage of a situation like that.

I'm not too fussed where we eat out – Edele's the fussy one! What I do hate are olives and smelly cheese. I love Indian food because they manage to make plain vegetables taste absolutely great. Italian food eaten in Italy is amazing! We'd performed with The Corrs and Natalie Imbruglia at a fashion show in Rome, then dined that night on authentic fresh Italian ravioli which was a great experience.

In our job we often have to eat very quickly, which is not good for our metabolism. I'd been to see an acupuncturist because my energy was low and was taken off sugar (surprisingly) and given a whole load of things, including a product for the digestive system, acidophilus, which really helps. I also take Vitamin C regularly.

Going to the movies is a pastime we all enjoy. Lindsay and I managed to see *Notting Hill* and loved it. *Dirty Dancing* is my all-time favourite film and I could watch it over and over again. My favourite actors are Gwyneth Paltrow and Samuel L. Jackson. I enjoy reading Danielle Steele novels or listening to Robbie Williams, The Corrs, Lauryn Hill, Savage Garden and Chicago, although they're an older band. My favourite soloists are Diana Ross and George Michael.

I have the fairest skin out of the four of us so don't like sitting in the sun for very long. If I do then I put on loads of protection. I just don't like the idea of getting burnt. I have been on sunbeds in the past, but would never do it now. I once went to the Bahamas, but found it too hot – I enjoy a breeze. Given the choice I think I'd prefer to holiday somewhere more scenic than hot.

Chapter 4
On the Road Survival Guide

Nobody and nothing could have ever prepared us for life on the road. It's been an incredible learning experience from which we have all benefited professionally and personally. When the going gets tough, it's the support of our families, friends, colleagues and fans which keeps us going.

Above all, it's vital to have a sense of humour! Like the time our tour bus broke down and we had to go on to the venue by car. When we arrived we realized we'd left everything on the bus! It got closer and closer to the time we had to go on and there we were borrowing clothes from co-star Tatyana Ali. The 'N Sync sound people helped us out with sound and everyone rallied round. It was also the night that our recording company had flown out to watch. We thought it would be a disaster, but the audience didn't have a clue that anything was wrong!

'The hostess simply couldn't understand why Sinéad slept for twenty-two hours out of the 24-hour flight!'

Technical hitches are few and far between, because we have such a competent sound team, but we do sometimes have to get out of tricky situations.

It took a little while to get used to wearing the in-ear monitors which help us when performing live. One time, Edele's ear monitor pack went down on stage and when she put on the spare pack it was picking up radio station frequencies and she found herself listening to music from a local radio station!

One of the hand signals, which means to turn up the track in our ear-monitors, is also one of the dance moves in

'Rollercoaster,' so for a few days our sound man, Steve, was confused because Edele wanted the level changed at the same time every night!

Although we wear the in-ear monitors, we are not completely oblivious to other sounds in the venue. Sometimes we get problems with the PA sound bouncing off the back wall and there can be a fraction of a second delay, which can be quite confusing.

Over the past two years we've become much better at handling the press. We don't often get the chance to see what's been written about us, but in general we seem to get very good write-ups. In the early days, we were given a few pointers about how to handle certain types of question, but when it comes to the crunch, you have to deal with every situation as it arises.

We do a lot of 'phoners,' which means reporters speak to us on our mobile phones while we're in a car or on the tour bus. It's the only way they will catch us. It can be annoying when you chat with someone for maybe just half an hour and they are able to pass judgement on you as if they've known you all your life, but if we took to heart everything that was written about us we'd go crazy! And as for some of the questions we sometimes get asked! It'll take a lot to beat, 'What's the sexiest Alien you've ever met?!'

Reach for the Skies

Plane-hopping has become a way of life in recent months. We couldn't begin to recall how many hours we've spent in airports or the number of flights we've taken. Fortunately, none of us are nervous flyers and usually make the most of our air time to catch up on some sleep! When we went to Australia last year we'd just done a 24-hour shoot for 'To You I Belong.' The hostess simply couldn't understand why Sinéad slept for twenty-two hours out of the 24-hour flight!

LINDSAY

I hate airports. I hate having to check in and rush for the gate. I didn't mind in the beginning but when we're in America we can end up taking an average of four flights a day. I'd swap a plane for our tour bus any day.

We do tend to get portrayed as 'good girls' who don't do this and don't do that. At the end of the day we are just four normal people who work hard for a living. When we go home to our families and friends then of course we like to go out! It was pleasing to get a write-up in the *Daily Telegraph*, one of Britain's quality daily papers.

There is rarely a day when we don't do any travelling and it can be really awkward when you're trying to get in touch with people back home. That's why I always have my watch set by British time. Nowadays, I don't even bother to unpack properly at the other end. I just take out what I need because, before you know it, you're on the move again.

I usually use a hard suitcase and for some reason have a habit of packing my trousers at the back and tops at the front. Our denim show costumes are all packed separately by our wardrobe lady, Marian. My flight bag includes: Discman, CDs, book, Filofax, tickets, chewing gum, phone, wallet, passport – nothing out of the ordinary. As soon as we take off I'm ready to zonk out!

I help myself to avoid too much jetlag on long-haul flights by getting prepared a couple of days before. I work out what time it's going to be in that country then adjust my sleeping hours accordingly. I may go to bed later two days before, then even later the day before, so that there is not such a dramatic change. Other than that, I just go with the flow. It looks as if we might get to fly to New York with Concorde in the autumn – it only takes about three hours and we could be there and back in a day with no real jetlag.

B EDELE

It makes all the difference in the world if you can get to sleep on a long-haul flight. And I wouldn't travel anywhere without my turquoise pillow, which was designed by my nephew, Dean, and made up by my mam. I take it everywhere – especially on planes! My teddy bear, Patch, goes too.

You'll always find moisturizer and hand cream in my flight bag, which I put on about every half hour because the journey dehydrates your skin. When drinks are offered, I'll choose either water or tomato juice. I'm forever spilling the tomato juice and it never comes out so now I make sure I've got something to change into.

If I'm not snoozing, I'll listen to my Walkman, watch telly or read. In fact I prefer to sleep in the airport lounge rather than look round the shops.

I still can't manage to travel light and always end up taking far more than I need. I'll take things I won't even wear – I just like to have the option. When we first moved to England I had all my clothes in one bag which fell off the baggage train between the plane and the terminal. All my clothes were ripped to shreds! The contents were worth around £1,500 and I only got back £300. I had to dash out and buy a jumper and two pairs of trousers. In fact, I'm still topping up my wardrobe from that incident.

We normally travel business class and on very special occasions get to fly by private jet. Our record company put us on one for a conference in Key West – what luxury! The only thing with private planes is they don't always have a toilet. Sometimes the toilet is under a seat and you have to pull a curtain across for privacy, then everyone's too embarrassed to go! Now we won't get on a plane unless it's got a proper toilet.

Jetlag is always worse on the return journey than going out. LA back to Britain is a killer and can take you about two days to recuperate.

SINÉAD

It's great when you get an airport where you don't need to show a boarding pass and you can go straight through, otherwise you've got to stand in line, which I don't like.

I'll never forget that flight to Australia when I slept most of the way. But I'm afraid sleep is the only thing a B*Witched member wants to do when you follow a schedule like ours. I'm not generally a nervous flyer but a while back an American plane crashed and it belonged to one of the airlines we use a lot. That was the first time I ever thought, What if?

I'm like Edele in that I always take far too many clothes and just cannot decide what to leave out of my suitcase. My clothes go in one case and I have a wheely bag for toiletries, towels, bits and bobs — things that I want to get out easily.

My hand luggage consists of phone, filofax, sunglasses, a little bit of make-up, CD player and some CDs. I don't like reading on a plane, but do read a lot on the tour bus.

Aeroplane food can be pleasantly surprising, especially if you are flying business class, which we always do. The return flight to Britain from the States is great when you can get good old Cheddar cheese!

KEAVY

There's really nothing glamorous about jetting in and out of different airports. I actually get bored - even in a VIP lounge! I've discovered fantastic hot chocolate in Starbucks, in US airports.

I took two suitcases when we went to the States for two and a half months earlier in the year, which was a ridiculous amount of luggage. My flight bag is easier to pack. I always take a dictaphone on board (you never know when a new song idea might come into your head!), my wallet and phone. You'll probably find some Dune perfume by Christian Dior, deodorant, photos of my family and friends and some Nurofen headache pills — someone always needs those! Finally, I travel nowhere without my crucifix, given to us by Sinéad's parents and my own.

I do have one request of the girls when we're flying and that is for me to be allowed to sit on the left. Whether I'm dancing, walking or whatever I feel more comfortable on the left! I'd even go so far as to panic if I was on the right. I didn't even realize I was doing it until I went shopping with my mam. She said she wanted to walk on the left and we realized we both did it! Does that mean we can't go shopping together anymore?

Hotel Hotline

There's not a hotel room in the world that could take the place of our own bedrooms with their comfy beds and personal possessions. However, we do have some favourites, including an Irish-run hotel in New York, which is always ringing with the sound of familiar Irish accents. And it's always nice to return to the same hotels because the staff remember you and you get a nice welcome.

Unfortunately our mobile phones don't work in the States so we buy these special phone cards with which you can enter your code and dial normally. When it runs out, you just buy another.

- *Rule number two* - bring your own English teabags. Tea around the rest of the world is nothing in comparison.
- *Rule number three* – take something that reminds you of home.

- *Rule number one* is, without doubt, don't use hotel phones! With the number of calls the four of us make to Ireland, England and Greece we'd be bankrupt by now if we'd phoned direct from hotels all the time.

- *Rule number four* – always bring your own shampoo and conditioner. Never rely on those supplied in a hotel.
- *Rule number five* – take your own music in the form of a Walkman or Discman and a stack of CDs.

SINÉAD

People say they'd find it impossible to live out of a suitcase for the length of time that we sometimes have to, but I have to say it doesn't really bother me. It's nice when we can stay in a hotel for a few days in a row, as you need quite a lot of energy to keep packing and unpacking!

The only really frustrating thing would be the room service in Europe – you can't get anything after 11 p.m., which if you've just arrived is extremely annoying. In the States, however, room service runs throughout the night.

Sometimes the housekeeping staff just come in when you're least expecting it – to check your mini-bar or something. I remember in Vancouver, Edele was not feeling too well and had put a 'Do Not Disturb' sign on the door so she could get some rest – so they rang her instead to see if she wanted her room cleaned!

I usually leave a few clothes about the room to make it feel more like home and always put my toiletries out.

My own advice as regards surviving hotel life is quite simply: eat well, sleep well and if you have trouble sleeping, take your own pillow.

KEAVY

One of my main grumbles about hotels in the States is that the room service staff are often foreign and don't understand what you are asking for! I might fancy something on the menu, for example, chicken in a cream sauce, but because I prefer plain food I wouldn't want the sauce. Would I be able to get simple chicken without sauce?!

I've got my own furry hot water bottle, which goes everywhere with me. It's called mad, after mam and dad, who gave it to me. It's very important to have something to remind you of family and friends back home.

The most stupid thing happened to me one night – I woke up and must have fallen out of bed. I felt a right wally!

LINDSAY

Room service bugs me too! A typical example is breakfast. You might order cornflakes and a cup of tea. The cornflakes arrive, plus hot water for the tea, but there's no milk, sugar or a spoon to eat them with!

My favourite hotel is one we use frequently in Los Angeles. There's a great atmosphere, we get on with the staff and the food is brilliant. LA is always sunny when we're there so we can relax by the pool and almost feel we're on holiday!

I always take a little picture frame with a photo of my family to put on the bedside table and Spiros, my teddy bear, goes with me everywhere. For a more homely feel, I spread out all my toiletries in the bathroom.

 E D E L E

If we're visiting a country for the first time our record company usually leaves flowers in our rooms, which is lovely. Unfortunately, we can't take the flowers with us so we normally give them to the hotel maids.

I think we've all, at some stage, managed to leave a swimsuit or bikini hanging on the back of a hotel door, but I've never left anything valuable.

I agree with Keavy, Lindsay and Sinéad that room service is the most disappointing part of any hotel stay. So are noisy ventilation systems and folding beds. In one room I had the bed folded out of the wardrobe and I just wouldn't sleep in it in case I got 'snapped up,' so I changed the room!

We generally prefer to have our own rooms, but one Halloween night in Australia we got together and started telling ghost stories. Edele and Sinéad had decided to stay in the same room as they were scared. Keavy had already gone to bed, but Lindsay thought she'd be brave and go to her own room. A bit later she came to the room wrapped in a dressing gown and hugging her pillow. It ended up with the three of us in one bed!

Doctor's Orders

 K E A V Y

Touch wood, no one has been seriously ill while we've been on tour. Marian, our wonderful wardrobe mistress, always seems to have an endless supply of headache pills or whatever, for emergencies.

Sinéad had to have her ankle X-rayed when we were in LA. She'd fallen and hurt it a couple of times before, but that night the Irish dancing in 'C'est La Vie' proved to be the final straw. She was in agony and had to sit out the song on the side of the stage. Fortunately, nothing was broken, but the X-ray did show up lots of scar tissue.

Earlier in the year Lindsay had a bad bout of flu and was taking antibiotics. When we arrived in the States, she started coughing again so got some cough medicine from the chemist. She took it for a couple of days but felt completely up in the clouds. It must have been a pretty strong concoction because she started to feel better as soon as she stopped taking it!

I had to have some special orthopaedic foot supports when we were in LA. As lead singer, Edele's worst fear is getting a cold or sore throat which will affect her voice. That's why we are all so strict about taking our vitamins, although we think the multi-vitamins you can buy probably confuse your system. Edele and I were recommended vitamin B complex, which includes eight essential nutrients.

car from our hotel to a concert and it would normally have blacked-out windows.

We've been across the English Channel on the Eurostar train, which is excellent. You're in France in no time and it doesn't feel at all claustrophobic.

We've never been on a helicopter, but it's something we'd love to do, especially dare-devil Keavy Lynch! We were booked to go on a helicopter flight over New York but it was cancelled at the last minute due to bad weather.

Ask Lindsay her opinion on New York cab drivers and she'll compare an average taxi-ride to a rollercoaster! She thinks they're crazy speed freaks with a death-wish and not very friendly with it!

On the Move

SINÉAD

It's rare that we use any other form of transport than a plane or a bus. If we go shopping we're usually on foot and make sure we're wearing comfortable runners. Sometimes we get a

Denim Days

EDELE

Youngsters around the globe quickly latched on to the B*Witched denim code of dress and we are constantly being thanked by parents for the image we convey. Kids can copy our

Make-up artist Lee Pearson uses up yet more supplies of purple lipstick on Keavy

style just by putting on a pair of jeans and sprinkling a little glitter around and at very little cost!

It's a tremendous encouragement for us to hear comments like this and fans will be delighted to know that before long, we should have our own clothes' line bearing the B*Witched label.

You can imagine how thrilled we feel when we see so many fans in the audience dressed in denim!

Our stylist, Faye Sawyer, is amazing. She keeps coming up with these really unusual ways of working with denim, like the way she combined it with leather for our American video of 'Rollercoaster.' And you're going to see another denim twist in our 'Jessie Hold On' video, where Faye has incorporated embroidery and mirrored sequins. We're always looking for something original.

But disaster can strike when you are least expecting it. A low-flying pigeon decided to go to the toilet on my beautiful 'Rollercoaster' costume and our stylist found it very hard to get the stain out. Worse still, my all-time favourite 'Weatherman' clothes ended up covered in oil stains after the video shoot and she wasn't able to wear them again!

We can't recall any make-up disasters, although we do have individual preferences when it comes to certain cosmetic items, and who better to give you an objective report than our fantastic make-up artist, Lee Pearson:

- 'Edele has a real thing about eye sockets. She's socket mad – even if the overall look doesn't need it!
- Sinéad's passion are lips. She loves big, strong lips with a darkish red colour on the inside. Where the other girls might smear on some Vaseline, Sinéad just can't!
- Keavy wants purple anything and everything. Purple eye shadow, purple lips, purple hair – you name it, she's obsessed with purple!
- Lindsay loves eyeliner. I've had to pull it out of her hands a few times! She also likes creamy blushers she can smudge around – and a fake tan.'

B*Witched's Ten Tour Commandments
*Thou shalt telephone home
frequently to keep in touch
Thou shalt take vitamins regularly
Thou shalt get plenty of sleep
Thou shalt eat properly and try not to skip meals
Thou shalt not forget moisturizer on the plane
Thou shalt try to go to the gym to make
yourself feel better
Thou shalt bring stacks of music for the tour bus
Thou shalt try and persuade your family to come and visit
Thou shalt not use hotel telephones
unless you want an overdraft
Thou shalt not wear high heels to go shopping*

Caught in the Act

🐧 LINDSAY

There's never a dull moment in the B*Witched camp. You never know just who's watching, listening or about to take a photo at an inopportune moment! Keavy was well and truly caught out when we snapped her washing her feet in the dressing room sink straight after a show. Edele never thought she'd appear in print cleaning her teeth. Sinéad was gob-smacked when we caught her scoffing again and I promise I'm not in the habit of kissing aeroplanes!

Jeff, our tour bus driver, and Edele are renowned for the bets they make with each other over a game of pool. If Edele loses, then she might have to make him coffee every morning for a week. One time Jeff lost he had to wear this ridiculous luminous green jacket. Then it was double or quits. When Edele lost he made her push a peanut through the full length of the bus with her nose, and when she did he had to wear glitter for a week. At one stage he finished up with glitter on – as well as that awful green jacket!

Ouch! Sinéad's fall during a performance in LA left her hopping mad!

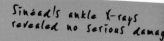

Sinéad's ankle x-rays revealed no serious damage

Stuffed again! Sinéad's always nibbling something!

The final touches!

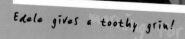

Edele gives a toothy grin!

t in the Act

LINDSAY

never a dull moment in the B*Witched camp. You
know just who's watching, listening or about to take a
at an inopportune moment! Keavy was well and truly
out when we sna
g room sink straight
appear in print cle
d when we caught
the habit of kissi

ur tour bus driver,
they make with eac
loses, then she migh
g for a week. One t
idiculous luminous gree
When Edele lost he
ll length of the bus
e had to wear glitte
d up with glitter on

It's a MAD life living out of a suitcase! And MAD is also the name of Keavy's furry friend

Lindsay takes some time out!

Lindsay thinks it's bliss when she
can travel by private plane!

Caught in the Act

Hug time - but don't get the sequence wrong!

Bus driver Jeff pays the price for losing to Edele at pool and gets smothered in glitter

feet first for Keavy!

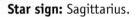

TRAVEL FACT FILE
KEAVY-JANE ELIZABETH
ANNIE LYNCH

Star sign: Sagittarius.

Distinguishing marks: I have a tattoo on my left shoulder blade.

Hair colour: Brown — but I'd love to have purple hair!

Eyes, height and shoe size: Identical to my twin sister.

Do you speak any foreign languages? I'm excellent at English, American and Canadian (Ha!). I speak a little bit of French, Irish and Portuguese.

Favourite foreign expression: 'Ela,' which is Greek. It means a few different things so I know a lot more Greek than I think I do!

Most interesting country visited: Japan is really different. It's interesting to see how a country could be so different to another one.

Favourite means of transport: A Golf GTI which I had — I loved it. I've been driving for about two and a half years but only have a provisional licence. I keep having to cancel my test date because of work. My dad often says to me I can get my Porsche soon, and I'm like I want my GTI back and he laughs.

Worst ever travel experience: In the early days of B*Witched we did a nightclub gig in Blackpool. On the way home we were stuck in a car in a traffic jam for about eight hours!

Funniest travel story: Once our tour bus broke down and we had to do a gig with no costumes and no sound guys. That was funny!

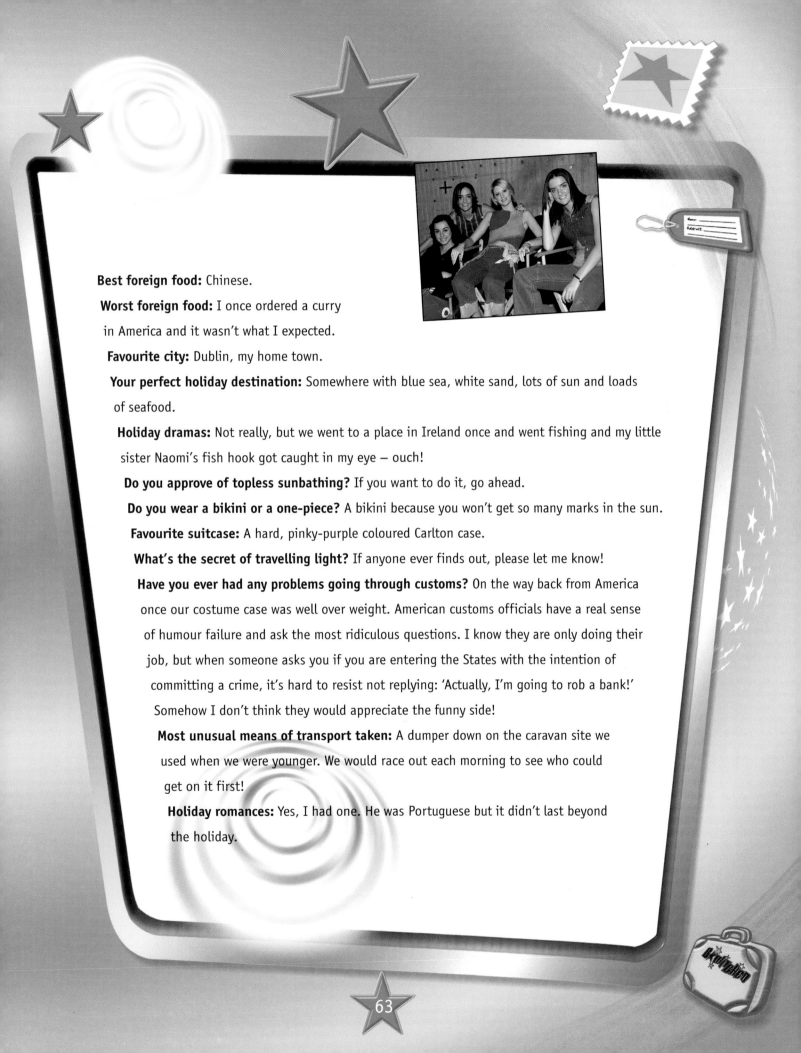

Best foreign food: Chinese.

Worst foreign food: I once ordered a curry in America and it wasn't what I expected.

Favourite city: Dublin, my home town.

Your perfect holiday destination: Somewhere with blue sea, white sand, lots of sun and loads of seafood.

Holiday dramas: Not really, but we went to a place in Ireland once and went fishing and my little sister Naomi's fish hook got caught in my eye – ouch!

Do you approve of topless sunbathing? If you want to do it, go ahead.

Do you wear a bikini or a one-piece? A bikini because you won't get so many marks in the sun.

Favourite suitcase: A hard, pinky-purple coloured Carlton case.

What's the secret of travelling light? If anyone ever finds out, please let me know!

Have you ever had any problems going through customs? On the way back from America once our costume case was well over weight. American customs officials have a real sense of humour failure and ask the most ridiculous questions. I know they are only doing their job, but when someone asks you if you are entering the States with the intention of committing a crime, it's hard to resist not replying: 'Actually, I'm going to rob a bank!' Somehow I don't think they would appreciate the funny side!

Most unusual means of transport taken: A dumper down on the caravan site we used when we were younger. We would race out each morning to see who could get on it first!

Holiday romances: Yes, I had one. He was Portuguese but it didn't last beyond the holiday.

Chapter 5
Home Thoughts from Abroad

Never a single day goes by when we're on tour when we don't think about our families and friends back home. When we're working flat out, our minds are completely focused on doing our job well but at the end of the day our thoughts usually turn towards home.

That's why it was so wonderful when Sony offered to fly out our parents to join us on a leg of our US tour in March. You can imagine the excitement as we warmed up on stage and turned round to see our mams and dads standing there!

Although we four girls are extremely fond of each other, we still love the contact with our families and old friends, so it's always nice when they keep in touch and bring us up to date with what's going on back home.

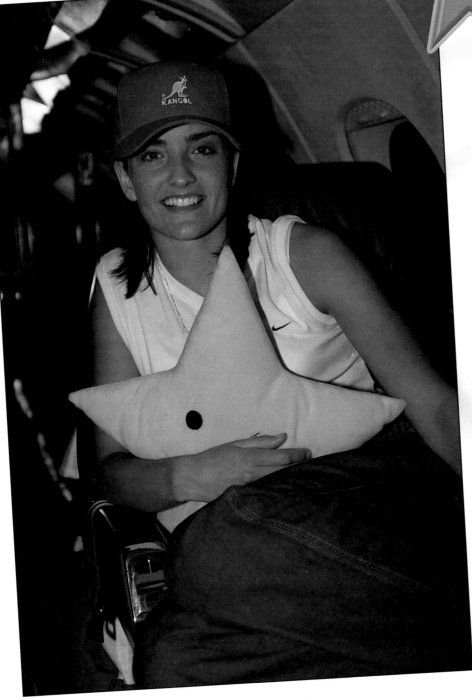

But the more you go away, the more you get used to it. The hardest part is leaving again after each trip home. And I can't imagine ever getting so used to being away that I wouldn't want to go home.

Naturally, I spend a lot of time on the phone – thank heaven for mobiles. I phone mam and dad every chance I get, even if it's just to say, 'Hi!'. Our phone bills were big enough before we started touring, so I dare not tell you what they come to now!

I wouldn't swap any aspect of my B*Witched life for the world, but you do miss having people to talk to. You might not believe it, but you can be surrounded by lots of people and still get lonely – that's how I feel sometimes.

It was fabulous when Sony flew out our parents and my sister, Naomi, for part of the US tour. We had an idea that they were going to join us at some stage, but we were completely caught off guard when they turned up. My parents were also trying to surprise my older sister, Allison, who works near Boston – only she nearly decided to fly home to Ireland for a few days that week, which would have really messed things up!

 K E A V Y

When the band was taken on by English management and we moved to England, it was very hard for us at first. There's no way I could have gone alone – I used to cry after every call home.

I think it helped them to cope a bit better with our long absences by being able to meet all the people we talk about and by seeing things like the tour bus for themselves.

In some ways being away might be slightly easier for Edele and me. At least I have part of my family with me all the time. I hate it if she ever goes away and fortunately it's only ever happened twice. I feel she is such a part of me — it's really strange when she goes. I think if she ever went solo, I'd be her wardrobe girl!

What do I miss most about home? Definitely my bed! It's so weird getting used to strange beds nearly every night. If I could bring my own mattress and pillow, it would be wonderful.

We have a very large family. Edele and I are two of six children and we all live in different places. As a result, it's often extremely difficult to get the whole family in one place at the same time. So far Edele and I haven't missed out on many major family events, although we weren't there for our dad's fiftieth birthday this year, which was sad.

Last New Year we'd just arrived in California and it was the first time we'd spent New Year away from home. I remember we sat in our hotel room in Las Vegas and cried. We couldn't even phone at midnight British time because we were on a plane.

 LINDSAY

It's surprising how time flies by when we're on the road and on a 'mission' so to speak. The only time I ever feel homesick is when we have a day or an evening off.

Mostly I miss my friends and family and just being in familiar surroundings. As I grew up in Greece and moved to Ireland when I was thirteen, I suppose I have two places I call home, yet I tend to think of home as being wherever my family is.

I'm an only child, but I don't think that makes it any harder or easier to cope with homesickness. Nothing can prepare you for it and you have to expect it. We all phone home as often as we can and I'm actually pretty good at sending postcards from different places.

'You can imagine the excitement as we warmed up on stage and turned round to see our mams and dads standing there!'

69

I've missed four of my friends' twenty-first birthdays, which is annoying, but can't be avoided. The good thing is that true friends accept that it's impossible for us to attend all these special celebrations and so they never make you feel bad about it.

I love being home for Christmas and the past couple of years I've spent it with my family in Greece. I was raised a Catholic and so we do the normal things like going to church in the morning on Christmas Day. Basically, we celebrate Christmas as we would in Ireland by opening presents in the morning and having a turkey dinner later on. There is a special Greek Christmas speciality that I adore, called *kouabiethes* — these are kind of nut-filled cookies, with a wonderful white powdery sugar coating.

 SINÉAD

I have to confess, I don't really get that homesick although there are days when I'd love nothing more than to be at home doing my own thing.

What do my parents worry most about while I'm away? Well, I think they want to know that I'm all right and that I'm eating well and I know they miss me but that they are also very proud of what we have achieved so far.

Unlike Keavy, Edele and Lindsay, I had lived in London before B*Witched, so I don't think it was as difficult for me to adapt. At first the others would probably cry and be upset because they missed everyone so much, but I think they are better now.

I think you just have to try and get through it yourself somehow — everyone handles it differently. I've tried to be as supportive as I can for the others.

I know my parents worry most when I'm on tour, but at the end of the day they know that we are surrounded by really nice people and that we are being well looked after. Now that they've met everybody we work with, I think it's far easier for them.

Although we've spent some of our longest periods ever overseas this year, I think we've actually had more time off in between. Last summer we only managed a four-day break for holidays, whereas this year we got two weeks.

I'll never forget the excitement when my parents turned up in New York. I knew a visit was on the cards, but thought it wouldn't be for a while yet. We'd been discussing among ourselves which would be the best leg of the tour for them to join us on. In the end they took us completely by surprise! I remember we'd just come off stage from a soundcheck and I saw Keavy and Edele's sister, Naomi. They travelled with us on the tour bus for the next ten days — it was fantastic!

My dad had always wanted to go to New York for St. Patrick's Day and during this trip his dream came true! We were working in Long Island and staying in an Irish hotel which we all love. Everyone was in good spirits and I know it's something Dad will never forget!

The rest of my family (sisters Elaine and Ailish and brother Paul) have all got their own lives, but we like to get together for celebrations like Christmas and New Year. On Christmas Day we all go to Mass in the morning, then call in at my auntie's house for a drink. We have a turkey dinner with all the works, including wonderful sherry trifle, around 4 p.m., then sit back and watch TV or just talk.

I always think New Year is a big anti-climax and very over-rated. I'm not sure where I'll be for the millennium celebrations. Some friends are thinking of going to America, so I might end up there.

EDELE

Every time I go home, the homesickness gets worse! And the more frequently we go away, the more often we have to endure it.

I miss my family and friends, my own bed, good old Irish milk and sliced white bread!

Keeping in touch by phone, especially while we are in the States, can be a frustrating experience. Time zones and busy lines create all kinds of communication problems! I try to talk to my family and friends every day, but sometimes that doesn't happen.

Moving to England for the first time was a complete disaster for myself and Keavy. Every time we were on the phone to our family and friends, we couldn't stop crying. It's great for us that our sister, Allison, lives in the States and we always meet up if we're in her area.

We managed to get back to Dublin for our nephew's Communion in May, which was a big family celebration. Dean is only seven and found it hard to understand why we had to miss his birthday last year, as we've always spent it with him.

Cruisin' LA style – Lindsay drove the band round Beverly Hills in this cool Mustang

74

Chapter 6
Having A Fantastic Time!

To all our fans around the world, we'd like to say thanks a million for all your support. You've been absolutely brilliant and we wouldn't be here without you. All your letters have been fantastic, so keep them coming!

Due to our American commitments we haven't appeared live in Europe for a while, so we're naturally eager to make up for lost time and hope to be with you all soon.

We've got plenty of exciting projects lined up for the coming months and can't wait to share them with you.

If you hadn't already heard, we now have an official Fan Club, which you can write to at: B*Witched Fan Club, Dublin House, PO Box 20144, London W10 5FH.

Sorry that it's taken such a long time to get a club together, but we wanted to make sure you're going to get nothing but the best!

B*Witched tour tickets can be booked through several leading on-line box offices as well as in leading music stores. A couple of clicks on your computer mouse and you're winging your way to the magical world of B*Witched!

All Dolled Up!

Can you imagine having your very own B*Witched all-singing, all-talking doll? Well, we hope you'll be able to buy realistic versions of ourselves in the very near future.

We had to have a million and one photographs of our heads taken from every possible angle, in order to come up with a good likeness. We will be dressed in denim and you will be able to buy miniature copies of our own video outfits for the dolls. Thanks to technology, the dolls will have about three sentences from each of us, available at the press of a button.

Our merchandizing company has been busy for months now developing new ideas. Several computer software products are in the pipeline as well as our own clothing line bearing the B*Witched label and a stunning range of accessories. The year 2000 B*Witched Calendar will be on sale from September and there'll be all kinds of merchandize at our tour venues.

And for all those of you who have a home computer and access to the Internet, continue to log on to our official web site address: www.b-witched.com for up to date news, views and tour dates.

SINÉAD

It's always been our aim to have a properly run fan club and we hope that fans will be pleased with our set-up. Fans need somewhere they can write to and where they can get correct information, otherwise they become disinterested.

I feel B*Witched's appeal lies essentially in the fact that fans think they could be like us. We definitely convey a 'girl next door' image, but that's exactly what we are — everyone started out as being a girl next door!

We don't walk around bragging that we are superstars and I think kids know that. We're four ordinary girls who went to school, loved dancing and singing and shared the same dreams and ambitions and have managed to fulfil them. That's the bottom line!

Our fans are usually very well behaved and never give us a hard time, for which we are extremely grateful. Some go to greater extremes to get to see us than others, like one group of English fans who follow us everywhere — girls, you know who you are! They appear at radio road shows and pop up at early morning TV shows and appear to know our timetable better than we do!

'How can we thank you enough for the letters you write and all the support you keep giving us.' (Keavy)

So far, our privacy has not been destroyed by persistent autograph hunters. Out of the four of us I think I would be the most difficult to recognize if I was alone and I certainly wouldn't make a point of letting on who I was. None of us looks for attention in that way.

Was I ever a fan of any pop star? I loved Wham! and still do like George Michael. Five Star was the only group I ever went to see in concert and I used to collect some bits and bobs about them.

We're really excited about all the merchandise that is coming out – especially the dolls. Imagine walking into a child's bedroom and finding it full of B*Witched memorabilia like bedspreads and pencil cases – that would be crazy!

KEAVY

Without the support of our fans around the world we would never have got where we are today. Our music is there to make you happy – so keep listening! How can we thank you enough for the letters you write and all the support you keep giving us.

I'll never forget a group of Swedish fans who met us at the airport and offered us garlands of flowers! It can be horrible to walk into strange, foreign airports so it was a wonderful feeling to be welcomed in that way.

We seem to appeal to so many people across so many ages because they can see that we have fun and enjoy what we are doing! And there's the energy we release – it makes the fans feel part of our show, and so they're not just spectators.

We all have a couple of fans back home who are constantly ringing our record company to find out where we are and often turn up at Dublin airport. They found out about our flight once and pretended to be our sisters. We went to the check-in and were told 'our other sister' had already checked in. We didn't know what on earth was going on!

We always stop whenever we can to sign autographs. Some fans get annoyed if we don't have time, but that's not very often. Others are positively mad and will stand in the rain for hours just to meet us!

If I'm signing an autograph I try and keep my signature consistent. If I changed it in any way someone might look at it and think it wasn't genuine.

We have quite a few people knocking on our door in Ireland and it's usually my mam who's there to answer. She's really good if there's a letter sent to the house. She'll always send them back an autograph and try and get us to sign their CD cases and posters — if they've sent them to us with a stamped addressed envelope, otherwise it would cost her a fortune!

Fans give us all kinds of presents, from socks and chocolates to bags and teddy bears. One girl gave Edele a denim jacket. We feel bad and often embarrassed that they spend their money on us but it seems to be their way of saying thank you for what we do.

 EDELE

Our fans don't really differ from one country to the next — they all have one thing in common and that's wanting to have a good time!

When we went to Singapore the fans were crazy. A group of twenty girls hired cabs for the day and followed us from the airport. There we were travelling through the streets of Singapore with a fleet of seven taxis in pursuit! The least we could do was to sign autographs when we reached our hotel.

We'd never try and avoid fans. For many of them it is the only time they are going to meet us, so we like to meet them. When people are getting our autographs, we sometimes get very strange requests. We once signed a baby's nappy and have even been cornered in toilets plenty of times!

I've never really been a huge fan of anybody, just music in general. I remember going to a *Smash Hits* concert a few years ago and seeing lots of different acts and wishing I could be on stage too. You can imagine how I felt when B*Witched appeared at a *Smash Hits* gig a couple of years later!

We are always keen to support worthy charitable causes and our mams are often asked for articles of our clothing or CDs to give for fund-raising auctions. We've done a couple of album compilations for national charities and we have also performed for the Prince's Trust in England.

Some people we know in Portugal are involved in a charity for abandoned dogs and we were more than happy to give our support to their cause as we hate to see animals being treated badly.

 **LINDSAY**

Apart from our music, I think fans like our energy. We do bounce around on stage a lot, which is very exhausting, but we never give anything but our best. Hopefully, they like us for who we are! They seem to admire us and look up to our music. Our audiences are all up for a good time. They sing, dance and scream along. It's the same wherever we go.

I enjoy meeting as many fans as I can and feel sorry for them if we are in a rush. We once had some fans fake backstage passes (perfectly!), but had to point out that it wasn't really the proper thing to do!

I grew up in Greece and no famous groups ever used to appear there, but I listened to pop music from an early age. I was a real New Kids On The Block fan and had their posters and albums. It was as if the singer knew he used to hang over my bed. I didn't get as far as asking for his autograph and if I had done, would probably have said it was for a little cousin!

In the early days of B*Witched we were doing some nightclub tours and I got asked to sign my autograph on a guy's stomach! There he was, really proud of his six-pack and I had to write on it!

No-one has my home address so any fan mail gets sent to Sony, although many fans hand over their letters in person. What sort of things do they write? They tell us how much they like us and our music and that we have given them inspiration to follow their dreams.

So many kids now have computers and they log on to our web site. We've done a few on-line chats through the site which is a great form of direct contact. They can ask us questions and get an immediate reply. It's a shame we don't have time to do more.

We never cease to be amazed at the response we get from fans in all corners of the globe. I was really shocked at the reception we got in Australia. It's so far away and yet the first day we arrived we went to Bondi Beach and people were snapping away with cameras and asking for autographs!

A couple of mall shows we did Down Under were packed out. We sang a couple of songs, got loads of teddy bears and other presents. One girl handed me a bag full of all kinds of little things. It means a lot to fans to be able to express their appreciation for the work we do, but we wish they wouldn't go spending their pocket money on us. Keavy was once given a watch and she was mortified!

TRAVEL FACT FILE
LINDSAY GAEL CHRISTIAN ARMAOU

Star sign: Sagittarius.

Nationality: Irish/Greek.

Distinguishing marks: Small scar from stitches under left side of upper lip.

Countries visited: Greece, Ireland, England, Spain, France, The Netherlands, Germany, Italy, Denmark, Belgium, Sweden, Finland, Switzerland, US, Canada, Japan, Singapore, Bangkok, Hong Kong, Australia and New Zealand.

Languages spoken: Fluent English and Greek and French quite well.

Favourite foreign expression: C'est la vie!

First trip abroad: From Greece to Ireland by plane when I was three months old.

Most interesting country visited: Japan — such a different culture and customs.

Favourite means of transport: Our US tour bus — I can just go to sleep in one of the bunks.

Worst travel experience: Getting four flights in one day and doing two shows in two different places. We were so tired!

Best foreign food eaten: Bay Bugs in Australia — something like small lobsters.

Worst foreign food eaten: Rice cakes in Japan.

Favourite city: Dublin – it's the friendliest and least tiring because it's small. It's also very cute!

Holiday dramas: I got bitten by a jellyfish once and it stung like mad! My mum rushed me to the chemist to get a special cream for it.

Do you approve of topless sunbathing: Different strokes for different folks! Just remember to put sunscreen on!

Do you prefer a bikini or a one-piece? Bikini – a brown belly is important!

Favourite suitcase: A big, blue hard case.

Is there a secret to travelling light? Don't bring things 'just in case'! Be realistic about needing things while you're away.

Do you have a driving licence? Yes, for about a year. I have a little Ford Fiesta in Greece. My favourite car is a two-seater sports Mercedes!

Are you a back-seat driver: No, but my mum is and it drives me mad!

Have you driven a car overseas? Apart from my car in Greece, I drove a convertible Mustang in LA for a Disney special we did. We were being filmed driving around so we had to go really slow and other drivers were getting impatient!

If you were shipwrecked and washed-up on a desert island, who would you want with you and which three possessions would you want? My best friend, my guitar, mobile phone and stereo.

Have you ever had a holiday romance?
Yes. He was Greek but it didn't last!

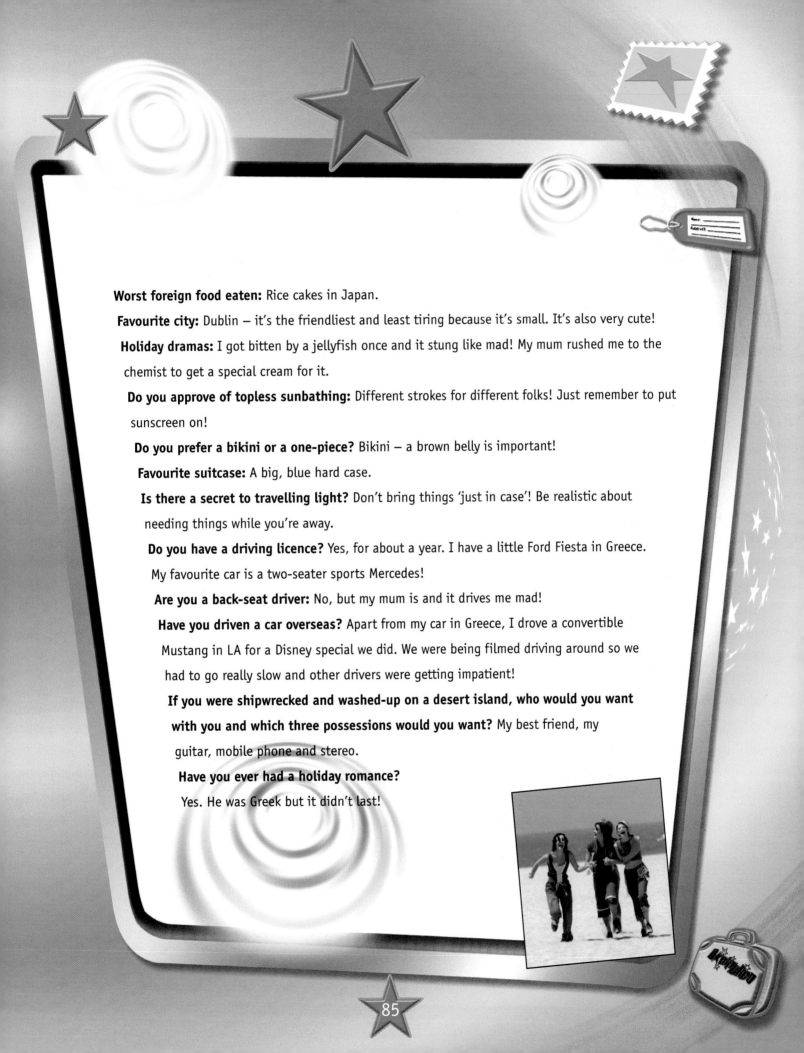

Chapter 7
Memories

We've visited so many foreign parts, seen so many incredible sights and performed in places beyond our wildest dreams. Each day brings along a pocketful of memories to remind us of life on the road. We'd like to share a few of them with you now, so sit back and take a trip with us down memory lane...

B EDELE

Our record company gave us a video camera as a joint present for the band and we try to use it whenever we can so that we have something to look back on when we get home. There should be plenty of footage for any home video we produce!

I have a camera but rarely use it and don't have time to keep a diary. My mam does her best to keep up a scrapbook of newspaper cuttings, magazine articles and photographs, but the more we do and the more places we visit, it gets very difficult.

Although we didn't spend much time there, Australia was really beautiful and I'll never forget it – the people, the climate, the animals, the food. Everything was lovely. We did a TV show on Elba Island, which is a stunning place and I'll never forget it either.

If I were to sum up the best moments of my career to date, it would be just the whole thing of performing on stage – something I've dreamed of since I was a small child. It's the best thing ever!

LINDSAY

I always kept a diary until about two years ago, but we became so busy I stopped. All I have now is a Filofax to jot down day-to-day things. I think I've got a copy of nearly every magazine we've been in and I try to take photographs of the many places we've been.

She leaves a videotape on record most of the day just in case we appear on any music programmes and although we usually know what's going to be aired a few weeks ahead, it's not easy to catch everything. Sony keep copies of all UK press write-ups but it's almost impossible to keep track of what's written about us outside the UK and Ireland.

One photograph is very special to me. I took it about two years ago when we were on the 911 tour. We drove by Wembley Arena the night before we were playing and saw our names as 911's guests outside on a big billboard. I felt so

excited. Looking at it now, we looked so young! In November our name will be up in lights again at Wembley, but this time for our own concert...I just can't wait!

Travelling in the US has been great and must feature among my favourite memories of 1999. To have broken the American market is such a great achievement and to have had four UK number one's in a row is unbelievable!

I thoroughly enjoyed dressing up in all the Abba gear for the BRIT Awards – we had such fun. Best of all, we had our first two-week holiday in about three years this summer and enjoyed a well-earned break!

In years to come, if I'm a granny and telling my grandchildren all about life in B*Witched, I think I'd tell them how well the four of us got on, how much we loved our job and that we'd managed to achieve our dreams together. I think we four will always stick together!

 KEAVY

Our video camera has come in useful for taping snatches of life backstage, of some of our signings or simply the wonderful scenery we've seen as our tour bus took us around the States.

I used to keep a personal diary but then found I didn't really like looking back at some of the comments and feelings I had written. It was really weird. Now, I'd rather just have the memories in my mind and details in my Filofax.

I have to confess I was rather 'snap-happy' when I first had a camera and when my last one broke, I didn't replace it. When we started sharing a flat in England I took so many photos that first day. If someone was cooking, then I'd take a photo of the cooker and so on. The girls thought I was bonkers! Now I'm really lazy.

My best B*Witched memory has to be when I got my first ever copy of our 'C'est La Vie' CD. I came home from work and it was lying in the doorway in an envelope. It was our CD and our song! Whether it was going to do well or not didn't matter. It was such an amazing feeling!

Performing live is what I love best and will remember for years to come. It doesn't matter how many people are in the audience. Whether it's a small-town shopping mall or a huge outdoor arena – I get the same thrill. I'll have so much to tell my children and grandchildren!

 ### SINÉAD

Buying small mementos of the places we've been helps me to remember what a good time we've had! In Japan I bought robes, tea, a tea set and a lantern and in Bangkok I picked up a nice little statue. When I get my own house it'll be lovely to have all these things around as constant reminders of my travels.

There's one photograph to date that will have pride of place on my mantelpiece and that's one of when we performed before Prince Charles at the Royal Variety Show. I haven't got an original from the show, but saw one in a magazine. I used to watch that show as a child so it meant so much to me to be there.

One day I'll tell my grandchildren about all the travelling and the different types of people I have met and would advise them to travel as well.

When I was young my own grandmother, on my mother's side, gave me this kind of advice. She told me not to think about boys – there'd be plenty of time for all that – and to get out and see the world! I really looked up to my grandmother. She always gave me great advice and I always feel that she's with me on my travels!

fancy That!

- Keavy is a blue-belt in kick-boxing, so watch out!

- Edele's favourite film is The Sound of Music.

- Lindsay was born in Athens, the capital city of Greece at 1.15 p.m. - just in time for lunch!

- Sinéad has a pair of grey French Connection trousers which she loves to wear when she's not working.

- Keavy would have no problem changing a flat tyre as she used to work in her dad Brendan's garage. And she'd be able to fix the puncture too!

- Green is Edele's favourite colour.

- Lindsay's favourite book is Sophie's World by Jostein Gaarder, which she finds deep and interesting.

- If Sinéad could have been in someone else's shoes, it would have been Mother Teresa's to see how she worked.

- The girls have specially designed B*Witched rings which they like to wear for good luck. They were given as a gift by Sony: Edele's has 'B' for B*Witched; Keavy's has the star from the band's logo; Sinéad's has a shamrock, which is Ireland's lucky charm and Lindsay's has a cat – she's mad about cats!

- Keavy's favourite film is Grease, starring John Travolta and Olivia Newton-John.

- Edele recommends Christian Dior concealer.

- Lindsay would love to have Shania Twain's hit 'From This Moment' played at her wedding as it's full of promises and vows for the future!

- Sinéad adores Motown music – it makes her want to have a good time!

- Keavy loves driving go-karts and has smashed into a few walls and tyres over the years.

- Edele's christening bracelet is her most sentimental jewellery item.

- Lindsay loves a 'glossy shiny thing' by L'Oreal, which she smudges on her cheekbones.

- Sinéad won school certificates for speech, drama, singing, piano and Irish dancing.

- Keavy was once 'a birthday present' for someone! She went to Spain for a few days and a friend asked her to be another friend's gift. Keavy felt really embarrassed but it made the girl's day and everyone was delighted!

- A roll of leather fabric used to wrap around the sleeves and tops of coats the band wore, is Edele's favourite clothing accessory.

- Lindsay loves belts – to hold up her baggy trousers!

- Sinéad would love to invite Jim Carrey and the cast from Friends for dinner for an eventful night full of surprises!

- Keavy uses a 'Sharpie' marker pen for signing autographs. She's signed everything from shoes to caps and pillow cases for fans!

- Edele and Keavy can water-ski and snow-ski.

- Lindsay's perfect dinner guests would be: Eric Clapton to serenade them with his guitar; Mariah Carey to sing; Patrick Swayze and Jennifer Grey so they could dance as they did in Dirty Dancing; Robbie Williams will 'entertain us!' and last but not least, the rest of B*Witched.

- We don't often get the chance to hear our own music, but we have been surprised to hear it in some unexpected places: Edele heard 'C'est La Vie' at a beach bar in Portugal; Keavy saw herself on a huge video screen in a Levi store, whereas Sinéad walked round the corner of a Dublin street to hear 'Blame It On The Weatherman' blaring out from an HMV store!

Chapter 8

Forever Friends

Friends make the world go round! We've never met four people who live and work together who get on so well as ourselves. We're four very different people and we respect that, but we do share a common goal — to make people happy through our music — and that has definitely helped to cement our relationship.

When we get any time off, we usually spend it together and rarely feel the need to go our separate ways. We genuinely care for each other.

But we can't imagine where we would we be today without the encouragement and support of our close friends back home. We may not get the chance to speak to them for days, but they understand our schedule and commitments and never get jealous or angry because of it. Of course, since we joined the band, we've all lost some friends along the way, but we realize now they were probably never true friends at all!

And we've made lots of new friends through B*Witched, especially among the people we work closely with like the tour crew, our management and our record company, our hairdresser, stylist and make-up artist.

We've met so many lovely people in far-flung parts whom we will probably never see again. They cross our lives for a few hours and then we have to move on, which is a shame.

None of us likes to talk about our own strengths and weaknesses, so we decided to give you a little insight into our characters by getting each band member to talk about the rest! Here we go...!

KEAVY

By Sinéad: Keavy's really funny and very ambitious. She's a great performer, is very spontaneous on stage and adores the fans. She is quite sensitive but very caring towards others. Keavy is the tidiest of the four of us – her room is always spotless and her case is always tidy. If she's passionate about something, she'll go for it!

By Edele: There's nothing like the relationship my twin sister and I have! It's definitely a unique bond. There's no way I'd be on the road without her. Keavy is great to have around – she's entertaining and keeps us all laughing. She's a very good listener too. My sister is a very talented singer and dancer who gives 150 per cent to anything she does. She's handy around the house and her own room is immaculate.

'We've met so many lovely people in far-flung parts whom we will probably never see again.'

By Lindsay: What a great friend! Keavy's funny, yet sensitive and quite daring. If there was a crazy rollercoaster to ride, then she'd be the one to egg everyone else on. She adores her work, is a perfectionist and is very focused and ambitious.

SINÉAD

By Keavy: Sinéad's both a good listener and talker. She had quite a different life, living more in the country, and left home before the rest of us. She's the sophisticated one, who loves to dress in classy black, wear high heels and feel made-up. Because of this she comes across as being older, yet to look at she looks younger as she's so petite. When she dances she moves so well. She might look more fragile, but she certainly gives it 'loads of attitude'! She's not particularly tidy and will admit this herself! Sinéad tells us all she can cook a wicked sherry trifle but we're still waiting for her to make it – hint, hint!

LINDSAY

By Edele: Definitely the sophisticated one! Sinéad's a very good person to talk to and an excellent listener. On stage she's very girly and glamorous and you can see that when she dances. She's very talented and ambitious. When we first moved to England, Sinéad was a great help when we were upset about being away from home, as she'd lived away from home before. She's got a weakness for collecting scented candles, which she keeps in her room.

By Lindsay: Sinéad is sophisticated and very ladylike. She's sensitive, a good listener, very daring and loves her desserts! She used to have the messiest room, but I have stolen that role from her recently, I think! She's the one who leaves things behind the most — and loses everything!

By Edele: She's the most laid-back out of us. If her phone rings, it takes her ages to get it out of her bag and she usually misses the call. Nothing worries her! She's never bothered how we are going to get somewhere — she just follows along. Her personality really comes over on stage. Everyone calls her the young, cute one! She's the one everyone fancies with her curly hair and she's always giggling! She's also very talented. Her room's a mess and she loves leaving empty cereal boxes in the cupboard!

By Keavy: Bubbly, laid-back and full of giggles — that's Lindsay. She's used to being away from home as she grew up first in Greece, then Ireland. Her laid-back attitude extends to the stage and this is where her real personality comes across.

'When she dances she moves so well. She might look more fragile, but she certainly gives it loads of attitude...!'
(Keavy on Sinéad)

By Sinéad: Lindsay can be quite private at times. She holds things very close to herself, like her family. If there was something on her mind she'd rather sort it out in her head to work out the best way of dealing with it. Lindsay is intelligent, creative and good at languages. She reads philosophy books and likes deep conversations. She has us in stitches on stage sometimes as she has this ability to suddenly burst into an American accent and we're like, 'What?'.

EDELE

By Lindsay: Edele will always give you good advice and tell you straight out what you want to know. She's very funny sometimes and quite sensible. She was the natural choice as our spokesperson and is marvellous at saying things on our behalf. In the same way, her voice was perfect for the role of lead vocalist – the best thing for B*Witched. She's very good at chores around the house – if someone's forgotten to clean the loo she'll tell you to do so!

By Keavy: I've always been able to talk to Edele and she's always been my best friend. I can always go to her for advice, even if I don't want to hear the right answer. She's so focused on what we are doing and why we are doing it. Our twin connection is very strong – I feel more for Edele sometimes than I do for myself!

By Sinéad: She's a born leader! She knows what she wants and says what she thinks – no matter what age the person is! She never bottles anything up inside and you always know where you stand with her. Edele has a fantastic voice and more than deserves to be our lead singer. She's definitely the best woman for the job! She's not quite as tidy as her sister, and would let her room get messy for a while before tidying it up.

Best of friends

SINÉAD

My close friend, Ciara, lives in San Francisco but our friendship, which was formed in college days in London, has never faltered. I can go for months without seeing her and we just take up where we left off. Another close friend, Shereen, lives in Dublin and when I'm back in town, we love nothing more than to get together, have a Chinese meal and a good natter.

KEAVY & EDELE

We shared many friendships while we were at school, but when boyfriends came on the scene we developed some separate relationships.

'I think a best friend is someone whom you can depend on.' (Sinéad)

Our really close friends like Peggie-Anne, Sandra, Joanne and Mark always understand if we can't keep in touch as often as we would like because of work. It can never be quite the same as before B*Witched, but we certainly all make up for lost time when we get together.

 LINDSAY

As I spent my childhood in Greece, where I was born, I'm lucky enough to have best friends in both Greece and Ireland. In Greece there's Melody, Julie, Theodora and Paula and in Ireland there's Grainne and Lorna, who are all very supportive of B*Witched. I phone them as often as I can and send postcards. When we finally get to meet up it's as though we've never been apart! There's never any awkwardness or silences. I spent several years at boarding school in Ireland and loved it because I felt I had sisters, even though I was an only child.

A Perfect friend...

 SINÉAD

I think a best friend is someone whom you can depend on. We all have different priorities and agendas, which we must respect. Neither one should mind the other doing their own thing.

 LINDSAY

The perfect friend should be someone who is on the same wavelength as yourself. They need to be able to laugh and not be jealous of what you do.

 KEAVY

Best friends should be really honest with each other and tell the truth. It's good to have someone who's a good listener and who can really be trusted.

 EDELE

Sometimes even best friends fall out – especially over boyfriends! If you do have a difference of opinion, you should always try to look at it from the other person's point of view.

'Forever Friends'

TRAVEL FACT FILE
SINÉAD MARIA O'CARROLL

Nationality: Irish.

Distinguishing marks: Scar on my forehead.

Hair: Blonde.

Eyes: Blue.

Shoe size: $4\frac{1}{2}$.

Languages spoken: English and French. I used to speak French quite fluently. I au-paired in Bordeaux for three months when I was in school, but now only speak a little.

Favourite foreign expression: Adios, amigos!

First trip abroad: I went to Wales by boat with my parents when I was about eight.

First flight: We went on holiday to Spain for two weeks. I was very excited about flying, but remember getting bored!

Most interesting country visited: Japan – it's so different. I bought a lot of authentic things.

Favourite means of transport: Our tour bus because we can sleep, eat and watch videos.

Favourite city visited: Vancouver.

Where in the world would you like to go for a long weekend? Italy. I love everything Italian. The men, women and children all dress beautifully. Rome is noisy, though, and everyone zooms around on mopeds!

Favourite holiday destination: The Bahamas — beautiful weather, people and beaches.

Your views on topless bathing? I wouldn't do it, but everyone to their own. I don't agree with exposing yourself so much.

What kind of suitcase do you use? I have two — one red and one yellow hardback as they're so durable.

What would you be most embarrassed about a custom's officer seeing in your suitcase if you were searched? My underwear!

Do you have a driving licence? Only a provisional one. I no longer have time to practice.

Favourite car: BMW convertible.

Could you change a tyre if you had a puncture? I'd have a good go!

Which form of transport would you love to travel on: Concorde — just to feel the speed of it. The Orient Express — for its luxurious sophistication!

If you were shipwrecked and washed-up on a desert island, who would you want as your companion and which three possessions would you want with you? My boyfriend, if I had one. My phone, stereo and CDs.

Have you ever had a holiday romance? No! I went on holiday with my parents when I was really young. I had my first kiss at fifteen and a half and from then on I was working every summer.

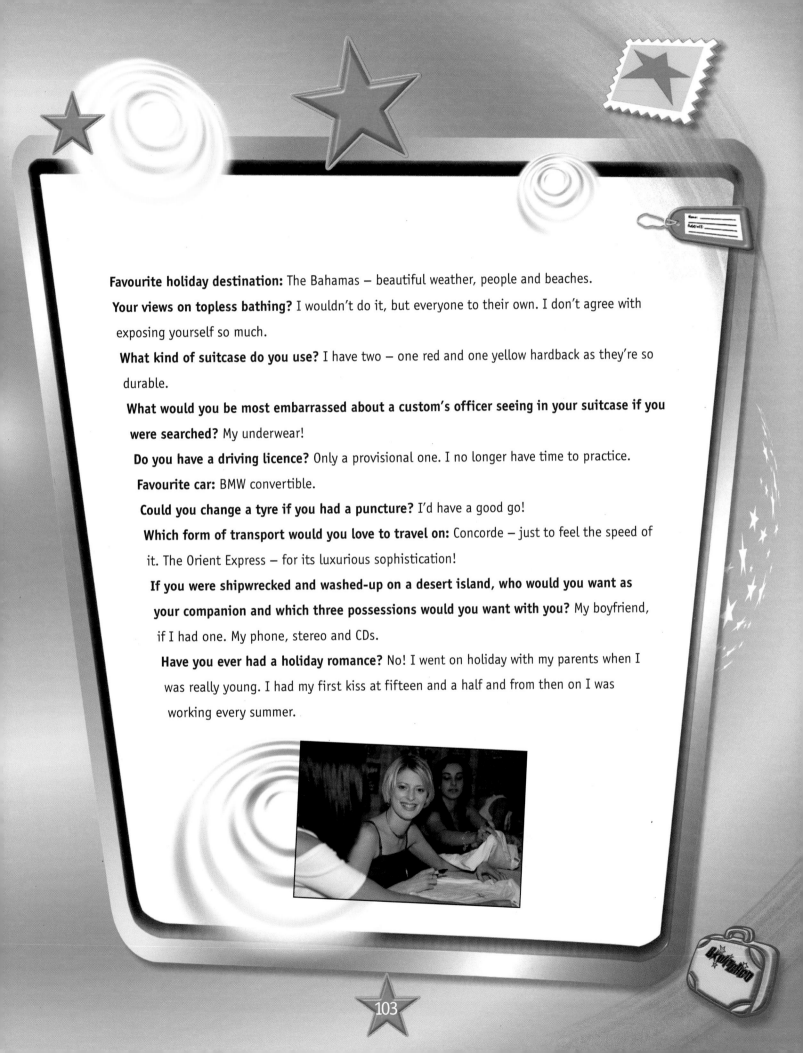

Chapter 9
In Dublin's Fair City

Ireland — the Emerald Isle — land of lush landscapes, rolling hills and fish-filled lakes — the country which, like a magnet, draws B*Witched back home!

In many respects, we are overseas 'ambassadors' for our country. We hope we represent everything that is good about our nation and through the Irish sounds in our music we maintain a strong link with our Celtic cultural heritage.

When an overseas trip is over, we happily hang up our dancing shoes, give our singing voices a rest, and return to the place we love best...

Irish milk and my mam's home cooking are what I miss most, so it's great to know I'm going to eat well for a week.

I'm very proud to be Irish and wouldn't want to be anything else. My earliest memory of Dublin, where I was born and raised, was a trip to Malahide Castle on the outskirts of the city. We used to go there lots as kids and buy green frog ice pops!

It's funny, but until I moved away and saw other capital cities, I'd never noticed that Dublin was such a beautiful city. We once did a photo shoot at Trinity College, which is the oldest university in the Republic of Ireland - that was a nice feeling.

KEAVY

The first thing I look forward to is getting a hug from mam and dad. Then sleeping in my own bed! I can't wait to see all my own friends and catch up with everyone. I just love relaxing at home — sitting in the house and having friends come to visit.

Café Mocha is my favourite city centre meeting place, where many pre-B*Witched days were spent discussing our hopes, dreams and ambitions over a cup of hot chocolate! I love shopping in the Liffey Valley shopping centre.

We had to study Irish language at school but I'm afraid I can't speak it as well as I'd like to. There are some all-Irish schools and a TV station, but it's not really spoken these days.

It did come in useful once during a family holiday to Portugal. My sisters Edele and Naomi and I went for a swim in a pool belonging to a big hotel. We got caught by one of the staff so we pretended that we couldn't speak English and reeled off some silly Irish expressions that we'd learned at school like, 'The goat is in the kitchen' and 'My mam is in the garden'!

 LINDSAY

I was born and grew up in Greece but spent many holidays with my mother and our Irish relations in Dublin. On those visits, I remember staying with my grandma and granddad and sharing a bed with my mum.

The first day we arrived in Ireland my mum wouldn't let me go out because I was tired from the journey, but for the rest of our stay, I'd play on the street with the local children. I'd always look forward to meeting up with them every year.

When I was thirteen, I came to live in Ireland permanently. I wasn't anxious about my new life at all because I already knew Ireland so well and as a person, I'm quite adaptable.

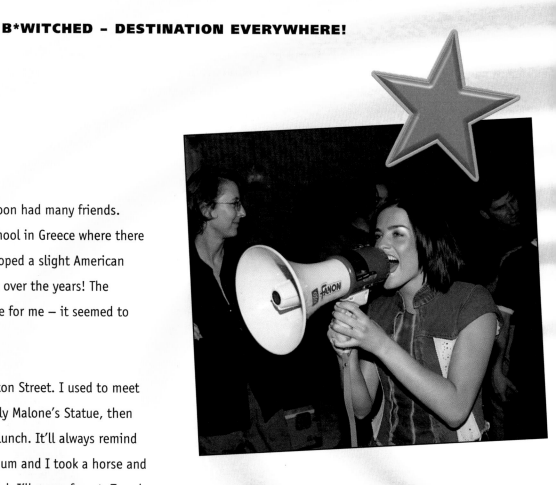

I fitted straight into school and soon had many friends. Because I'd been to an English school in Greece where there were many nationalities, I'd developed a slight American accent, but it's become more Irish over the years! The weather was the biggest difference for me – it seemed to rain the whole time!

I love walking down Dublin's Grafton Street. I used to meet all my friends on Saturdays at Molly Malone's Statue, then we'd go shopping and have some lunch. It'll always remind me of my friends. Years ago, my mum and I took a horse and carriage ride through the city, which I'll never forget. Temple Bar's also a great place, like a mini Camden Town, full of shops, cafés and bars. It has a cobbled street, is typically Irish and so cute.

We travelled around Ireland a fair bit on school trips and Galway, on the west coast, is gorgeous. Grainne, a good friend of mine, has a house in the country and is always inviting me to stay for a nice quiet weekend. I can't wait to go there. It's been a while since I've been able to spend some time with her and my other good friend, Lorna.

I'm extremely proud of my Greek roots too and can't think of a better combination. I love both countries just as much!

 **SINÉAD**

I grew up in Newbridge, County Kildare, about an hour's drive from Dublin. It used to be more rural and full of small communities – now we have bigger towns.

My grandfather used to take me on loads of drives into the mountains. I remember being down in Kerry and travelling on a horse and cart. We always went on holiday in Ireland – places like Sligo and Donegal on the west coast. I'd love to go up to the north coast of Ireland – I love the sea!

Dublin is a really colourful city. It's small by many city standards, but there are so many places to visit – it's very cosmopolitan. Temple Bar has such a diversity of restaurants and shops. Favourite of mine are Cooper's and Tosca and there's a fabulous Indian restaurant in Dalkey, called The Alminar. I love shopping in Morgan, French Connection and Airways.

I don't speak Irish very well and you'd really only need to if you wanted to work in radio or television in Ireland. It's great to be Irish — one of my earliest memories is of Irish dancing classes when I would be dressed in bright green! Wherever you've been brought up it's nice to see your country progressing in so many different areas. But I do think Ireland's history is very special.

EDELE

The flight is never quick enough home to Ireland. It always feels twice as long because you are so eager! When we get to the airport mam and dad have usually had some kind of welcome message entered into the announcement screen, like, 'Welcome home!' or 'B*Witched girls!'. As soon as I get in the door I run straight to the fridge for a glass of Avenmore full-fat milk and Brennan's Bread — it's just the best in the world. Then I go to my room to see if anything's changed — new covers or something on the wall, maybe.

We spent many childhood holidays at our caravan in Donabate. We'd play for hours in the rain, go and change into dry clothes, then go back outside again. Mam was constantly washing our clothes!

I like shopping on Grafton Street and love Blanchard's Shopping Centre. We do get spotted shopping in Dublin, but there's never so much hassle that we feel we can't go.

I learned far more about Ireland when I left. You really don't appreciate your home town when you are living there. There's a place called Power's Court, which has beautiful waterfalls and also a place called the Japanese Gardens and I've never been to either of them.

Speak Irish

Only a small number of people in Ireland speak Irish these days, although we all had to learn it in school. It's a Celtic language, which dates back hundreds of years and is very complicated to pronounce! Here are a few words to give you some idea of what we mean!

YES – *Sea* (pronounced *shah*)

PLEASE – *Le do thoil* (pronounced *leh doh hol*)

GOODBYE – *Slán leat* (pronounced *slarn lat*)

HELLO – *Dia dhuit* (pronounced *ah gwit*)

And how about this one for the name of the **PRIME MINISTER** of the Irish Republic – *Taoiseach* (pronounced *teeshack*)!

Did You Know?

• Our basic unit of currency is called the punt.

• St Patrick's Day on March 17 is our most important national holiday.

• Ireland is home to the famous Book of Kells – an illuminated manuscript of the Bible's Gospels and a wonderful example of Middle Age calligraphy.

• Hurling is one of our national sports – a fast and dangerous team game played with sticks called hurleys and a leather-covered cork ball, called a *sliothar*.

• Thousands of visitors a year go to Blarney Castle in Co. Cork to hang upside down and kiss the Blarney Stone, which is supposed to possess magical powers and give whoever kisses it persuasive powers of speech!

• Irish Dancing, which Sinéad did from an early age, is usually performed to music on the fiddle, harp and 'uillean' pipes. Two types of dance are the reels and the jigs, the jigs being more lively and more jerky.

• Textile manufacturing, especially linen and wool, is a very important industry for our country.

• Our nation's best known dish is Irish Stew, made with lamb or mutton which is simmered in hot water with potatoes, onions, carrots, leeks and pearl barley.

• Ireland is a well-known horse-breeding centre.

• The population of Ireland is under 4,000,000.

• At 220 miles, the Shannon is the longest river in Ireland and the British Isles.

Chapter 10
Into the Millennium

Looking Back

If only we knew what the future has in store! As we ride out the twentieth century and head into the twenty-first, we have big hopes that B*Witched is going to fulfill even more dreams, climb bigger mountains, achieve greater things.

No matter how much education you've had, no matter where you've come from and no matter what start you've had in life, if you work hard and are determined you can achieve anything. So remember, if you have a dream, work towards it. Believe in yourself and don't let anybody tell you that you can't do it.

From an early age all our lives had been filled with music, song and dance. We inherited many of these gifts from our ancestors and had the love, support and backing of our families to pursue our goals.

Our parents really believe in us and have been behind us since the beginning. We'd never be where we are today if they hadn't been. We had worked really hard together even before we had met our management or record company. Every spare minute we had, we spent rehearsing in the studio, working towards our dreams.

Music is one of the hardest industries to get into and one of the hardest to survive! Articles in the tabloid press and pop magazines may give many people the impression that musicians can become stars overnight, but that's definitely not the case! We spent months slogging away, working at night after our day jobs ended, in order to produce a look and a sound that would hopefully lead to bigger and better things.

Sinéad had a good deal of experience in the world of theatre and dance before we got together but even this did not prepare her for the feeling she had at our first show in the King's Hall, Belfast, when (as the group D'Zire) we were supporting Boyzone on tour. We were first on and the sheer thrill of standing before all these people was simply mind-blowing!

The events of the next few months are history now, but seem to remind us that if you really want something in life, you have to go for it. We've come a long way from the beginning, but we've never forgotten our simple wish to put a smile on your face.

Musical Directions

We've had great success with our singles and our album *B*Witched* and we've now got a second album on its way. So, B* assured, we intend to bring more joy and happiness to your lives through our music.

We've been working hard writing and recording to produce our second album, which will be released in the UK this autumn. And it's full of surprises. We've experimented with a lot of styles of music on this album. Our writing has really grown with our experiences and our time away from home. You will still see the Irish music in there, which is now one of our trademarks.

'Jessie Hold On,' the first single, is an up-tempo song with the influence of a banjo and we're really excited about it. We can't wait to release our new music so you can all hear it soon.

Another track, 'I Shall Be There,' was recorded with an African choir called Ladysmith Black Mambazo and it's absolutely beautiful. Definitely a sound to send shivers down the spine! We had a great afternoon recording with the choir. They were great fun to be with and the lead singer, Joseph, was doing some funky dance moves!

As you know, we co-wrote many of the songs on our first album and we have a great relationship with our producer, Ray 'Madman' Hedges. We've been extremely busy, but we've made time to have even more of a contribution to this album.

La Chat-Wich Cafe

We deliver!

L'escargot $4
Paté du merdre $5
truffle-wich $6
Beetlejuice $5
Fromagewich $3

We often get asked how we write songs. Well, there are never two ways alike. Would you believe it if we told you that the ideas for 'I Shall Be There' came together when we started messing around with a set of fridge magnets consisting of words used in romantic Elizabethan poetry?

One person might have an idea and everyone will work on it or it might be a collective thing from the start. There are so many aspects to song-writing, but what's important for us is that the four of us are well able to write, so we make the time to do so. We like to write about our own experiences and those around us.

'If you asked us a year ago we would never have even imagined that we'd be writing our own book...'

It's likely you may hear us playing instruments on our records in the future. We always love a new challenge and we are going to play our instruments on our tour. We're really excited about that!

The whole album has been a great adventure, which we'll never forget. Finding the time has been a nightmare! Due to our US tour schedule, we've had to find studio time here, there and everywhere. Some of our recording sessions took place in the car park studio of a LA hotel – we really love it there. We just hope none of us sound jetlagged on any of the tracks!

A little Advice from B*Witched...

 Keavy

You have to be prepared to work hard and if you are very serious, go for it! If you have a dream, follow it. Things will never happen if you sit back and wait for it. Grab the moment while you can. It's very important to have dreams and even better when you get to fulfill them!

Lindsay

Our lifestyle is not easy. You have to be very determined and work hard. Go for it and don't let anyone tell you that you are not talented!

Edele

Just remember, what goes around, comes around. So, be nice to people on the way up because you'll meet them on the way back down!

Sinéad

Don't be deceived by all the glitz and glamour. It's very hard work so make sure it's what you really want. Sleep well, take your vitamins and don't do too much partying. And if it doesn't work out, don't be too upset. Look at it logically – you know you can do something else.

Get Ready, Here We Come!

Every pop artist we know dreams of having his or her own concert. It's the perfect way to give something back to your fans. It's so exciting getting to choose your own support act, who will be on tour with you, and getting to put a whole show together.

So you can imagine how thrilled we were to hear that our greatest ambition so far is to be realized at the end of '99. We are going on tour and it's going to be a show to remember! We'd hate to spoil it for the fans who will be seeing us, so we're not going to reveal any of the secrets and surprises we have lined up. You'll just have to wait and see!

B EDELE

What we can tell you is that this will be the second chance our fans will get to see all four of us playing musical instruments. We did a 'Blame It On The Weatherman' acoustic session for MTV Live earlier in the year. I sang, Lindsay played the acoustic guitar, Sinéad played the accordion and Keavy was on tambourine and trap-cat (a kind of drum machine). We really enjoyed doing it and I think we surprised a lot of people!

On the tour we intend to play instruments on a couple of songs: Lindsay on guitar; Keavy on drums; Sinéad on keyboard and I'm going to try bass guitar, maybe.

Our stylist, hairdresser and make-up artist have all been incredibly busy since the first hint of a tour was mentioned. Our look will be undoubtedly denim, but there are bound to be a few new twists, which will take us into the next century. Their professional talents are likely to be stretched to the limit as we have a lot of other commitments to meet apart from the tour!

There's no place like home, so that's why we're going to start our tour at the Point theatre, Dublin, then it's straight across the Irish Sea to Newcastle. Yeah!

Where Do We Go from Here?

We're not planning on finishing up for a long time yet. We'll be together as long as you guys, our fans, want us and as long as we are enjoying it ourselves. There's still so much we want to achieve and there never seem to be enough hours in the day to get everything done.

If you asked us a year ago we would never have even imagined that we'd be writing our own book and here we are now, so who knows, there could be another in the New Year!

Our diary dates for the end of 1999 and the early part of 2000 are enough to keep you breathless. Apart from the tour, we are committed to a string of TV appearances along with radio, TV and press promotions across the UK and Europe.

Our tour will be the highlight of 1999 for us. For so long it felt miles away and by mid-summer we were already starting rehearsals with our choreographer, Shanie, in the States. I'm nervous and excited – all rolled into one! To be playing keyboard live is also a bit nerve-wracking. I studied piano for many years up to Grade Seven, but this is slightly different.

There are more plans to visit the States and we'll definitely be back in Australia. We'll be helping promote all the new merchandizing goodies as well – and that's just for starters!

 ### SINÉAD

It's so exciting to have a second album coming out. We've had far less time to record this one, but it will be just as B*witching. We're still involved in the writing side, which is very important to us and we hope next year will go just as well for us as this year, if not better!

It's been a great feeling for people all around the world to have been touched by our music. If I have children, I would never discourage them from a career in this business. I'd tell them everything I had learned and how it all was for me. It's always been important for me to know that my parents are behind me. You want them to be proud and to feel happy.

What will I be doing in five years' time? I never look that far ahead. Maybe I'll be a bit more settled and have my own house, but I've no real plans. Marriage and children do feature somewhere along the line, but if having the first is too painful, I might think before having another! In twenty years' time, I hope to be married with a family.

 ## L I N D S A Y

Our music is very different from any other band at the moment. We love to mix different styles of music together. The Irish music in an up-tempo song is very jolly and uplifting and in the ballads it's beautiful, serene and haunting. It's very important to have a difference and ours is our Irish music.

We've been privileged to meet such lovely people from all walks of life, including some very ill children whose last wish was to meet us. Those kinds of moment we'll never forget.

It has been very character-building being on the road. You have to put up with all kinds of things like homesickness and have to fend for yourself, but it makes you a stronger person. The whole thing is a learning experience and I've learned a lot in the past year about the business and life in general.

I'm very excited about the album and can't wait to get out there and promote our singles. As for our tour, well that's just incredible! And there's one thing I've set my heart on for the new millennium - I'm finally going to grow my hair!

In five years' time I hope we'll still be touring and promoting our music around the world and take B*Witched as far as we can go. As public figures, it's our job to cheer people up day by day and I'm fulfilling my dream by doing that.

 ## K E A V Y

I used to be called shy but now I can talk to new people a lot more than I used to be able to and it's all thanks to my work. We've all grown up since we've been travelling. We've met so many people, heard so many things and seen so much of the world. But it hasn't changed us as people — we're the same as when we started out.

I hope we'll continue to be so successful for years to come, but whatever happens to B*Witched, I can look back and see how well we've done compared to many others. We've made a lot of people smile and have influenced a lot of kids.

We get loads of letters from kids saying that if they are feeling down or distressed or have a problem, they put on one of our CDs and feel much better. To be able to do that for someone is great. One day we were working out in the gym and there was a man there who was working out to our CD. He said he loves to feel happy while he's working out and our CD was the perfect one to listen to!

Smile if you're feeling happy! A fan called Fiona gave Keavy this star-shaped pillow and it's been put to good use since

The most moving moment of my life with B*Witched to date still makes me proud when I think about it. We met a young American girl on tour who had cancer, only we didn't know it at the time. Her mam brought her to meet us and I'd given her a big hug. A few months later the lady asked our tour manager, Wilf, to say thanks to the girls, especially the one with the tattoo on her leg, which was me! She said all her daughter spoke about during the last few weeks of her life was that I'd given her a hug. It was overwhelmingly upsetting, but at least we'd helped to keep a smile on her face to the end.

> 'We've met so many people, heard so many things and seen so much of the world.' (Keavy)

We've had a lot of input into the next album. Most of the tracks are very different from the first album and it's the first time we've had anyone else record with us. It's the African choir, Ladysmith Black Mambazo, and they sing with us on 'I Shall Be There.' That was a real adventure!

For the tour we've suggested things that haven't been done before. We didn't want it to be just our concert, we want it to be a B*Witched spectacular!

Looking ahead, I'd like to think that I'd be married in about five years' time. I don't know if I'd be a good mother, but I'd like a large family like my own.

The millennium means just another New Year to me so I won't be doing anything any different than spending it with my family and friends. I've got so much to look forward to in 2000, including taking our tour to Australia and going to my sisters' double wedding next summer!

If my career with B*Witched ever ended I think I'd like to be a television presenter on one of the music or children's programmes. And at some stage, I'd love to do something with the other members of my family who are in the music business.

B EDELE

No words can describe the way I feel about having our own tour. Ever since the day the four of us met, we would imagine having our own concert. We're bursting with ideas and can't wait!

I hate looking too far ahead and like to live each day as it comes. You never know what is in store for you tomorrow. In the next few years I hope I'll still be in the music business and hopefully still with Keavy, Lindsay and Sinéad. We will perform together as long as people want us to.

I would love to get married, but there's plenty of time for that yet – maybe in the next five or ten years!

B*Witched Fan Club

- Do you know Sinéad's middle name?
- How did Edele get that scar on her nose?
- What did Keavy do before joining B*Witched?
- In what exotic place was Lindsay born?

For the answers to these and many, many more questions as well as all the latest news, gossip, gig details and exclusive photo's why not join the only official brand new B*Witched Fan Club! You'll receive a membership pack including a full size poster of B*Witched, picture cards of Edele, Keavy, Lindsay and Sinead, a membership card with your own unique number, a B*Witched folder and a special gift. In addition to this you will also receive four colour magazines in the year which not only keep you up-to-date with B*Witched but you will also have the chance to enter competitions and win fabulous prizes.

To join simply complete a photocopy of the form below and send it to us together with payment to the following address:

B*Witched Fan Club
Dublin House
PO Box 20144
London W10 5FH

To hear the latest message from B*Witched and regularly updated news why not call the Information Line

UK B*Witched Official Information Line — Tel: 0900 9 10 20 30

Calls cost 50p/min. Maximum cost £3.00. Please ask permission from the person who pays the bill.

Please use BLOCK CAPITALS:

Your Details   **MALE:**   **FEMALE:**

First name:

Surname:

Address:

City: Post/Zip Code:

Country: Tel No:

Email Address:

Date of Birth:

Payment Details...   UK & Ireland: £13.50   EEC: £15   Rest of the World: £19 or US$35

Please make cheques, postal orders and international money orders payable to B*Witched Fan Club. We look forward to sending you your B*Witched membership pack!

Author's Acknowledgements

Special thanks to: Edele, Keavy, Lindsay and Sinéad, Kim Glover, Doug Hurcombe, Maria Conroy, Vicky Kostura, Ailsa Robertson, Natasha Harding, the Lynch family and last, but not least, my husband Steve, my daughters Emma and Abby and my Mum.